CRYSTOPPERS

A PLAY BY PLAY GUIDE
FOR WISE PARENTING

Y. Aaron Kaweblum M.D. F.A.A.P.

authorHOUSE®

AuthorHouse™
1663 Liberty Drive
Bloomington, IN 47403
www.authorhouse.com
Phone: 1-800-839-8640

The purpose of this guide is to help you become successful parents, and to raise healthy, well balanced children/teenagers both physically and mentally.
The final decision regarding the implementation of the guidelines in this handbook should be between you and your health care provider.

First published by AuthorHouse   09/19/2011

ISBN: 978-1-4567-3102-1 (sc)
ISBN: 978-1-4567-3104-5 (hc)
ISBN: 978-1-4567-3103-8 (ebk)

Library of Congress Control Number: 2011902730

Printed in the United States of America

I dedicate this book first to my wife Yvette, my partner in life and my best friend. Yvette has supported and encouraged me since medical school and pediatric residencies in Mexico City and Miami. She was instrumental in raising our children and has been a guiding light in helping me become the best pediatrician I could be.

I also dedicate this book to our sons, daughters and grandchildren. I hope this parenting guide will help you succeed in your sacred mission of raising future generations of healthy, balanced and socially adapted children.

And finally, but not least, I dedicate my book to my patients' parents. Knowing that, so far, there is no such thing as "parenting school," I hope that this play-by-play parenting guide will help you successfully overcome the different and difficult obstacles you are going to face every step of the way in your parenting career.

Many people assisted me in producing this guide. Special thanks goes out to **Yael Ginsberg** for saving the day and doing a great professional job in reviewing and editing "Crystoppers." To my son and daughter-in-law, **Jonathan and Susie Kaweblum**, and to my good friends **Pat Padva** and **Linda Marcus** for their invaluable content input and feedback. Special thanks to my website designers, **Yael and Shlomo Sharoni** (http://www.sharoniz.com/), for their hard work and dedication.

Table Of Contents

Chapter I

INTRODUCTION

What is happening to discipline in this generation? What is happening to our teenagers? Why is it that we have the most unhealthy children in the entire world? Two thirds of our children are overweight. Our young adults have an unusually high incidence of heart disease, obesity, diabetes and chronic conditions that are the result of unhealthy habits because of poor parenting during the first years of life.

On top of the health risks of poor parenting, we are raising a generation of children unable to cope with frustrations. Children are aggressive, not only towards other children, but to their own parents. As an active pediatrician, I have even seen the emergence of a new social ailment, parental abuse.

For each unfortunate case of parents abusing their children, there are thousands of children abusing their parents. Society has created a mindset that makes parents think that it is a sin to allow a child to cry. As a result, parents stop parenting, and become "Crystoppers."

A Crystopper is a parent or parents who make important decisions regarding their children's care, health and well-being that are based solely on the parents' desire to make their children happy and appease them immediately.

The poor choices are the result of parenting decisions that are made only to stop the crying, screaming or tantrum that the child is in the middle of.

Crystopper decisions create an unhealthy relationship in which parents act and behave like servants, slaves or robots and not like wise guardians who create a loving and safe family that enables the child to grow emotionally, cognitively and physically.

NEED FOR WISE PARENTING

I have been a pediatrician since 1980. I have seen many physical illnesses. With new technology, medications and vaccinations, we have made significant progress in the improvement and maintenance of our children's health.

Medical students are taught everything possible about how to manage pediatric illness. Yet, they are taught very little about instructing parents in making wise decisions for their children. After practicing pediatric medicine for over 25 years, I decided to write this guide to help cultivate a culture of true parenting instead of parents who just react to their children's cries and therefore become Crystoppers.

Since the first years of a child's life, wise parents ensure that their children listen to them and do what they are told. Parents should be firm and loving and consistently guide their children to help them develop their individual gifts.

A wise parent follows three very simple rules:

1) If something is bad for your child DON'T DO IT, regardless of crying, whining, hugs, kisses or blackmail.
2) If something is good for your child DO IT, regardless of crying, whining, hugs kisses or blackmail.
3) Never say "I will try." If something needs to be done, DO IT. Like Yoda said: "do or do not, there is no try."

DIVORCE AND CRYSTOPPING

The following chapters will discuss the consequences on a child's life of being a Crystopper instead of being wise parents. In addition to the immediate consequences, very few consider the effects of Crystopper behavior on a marriage.

When a couple decides to get married, with all the good intentions and expectation that they will "grow old together," they believe that having a baby will bring them closer together, and serve to strengthen their relationship.

But even the typical demands of child-raising can distract parents from the needs of one another. Suffice it to say, when one parent is devoting 110% to their child's every wish and command, their attendance to the needs of their spouse will most assuredly suffer. Devoting that much attention is not only a drain on the parent's time but his energy as well, leaving nothing for his spouse. The effect of this is often resentment, and in some cases jealousy, of the attention given to the child.

A classic example of this phenomenon is allowing a child to sleep in the parents' bed for an extended period of time. While it will most assuredly appease the child, it severely interferes with couple's privacy and intimacy.

Children need and deserve attention, love and guidance. However, if parents don't agree with one another, there cannot be true love.

When a parent becomes a Crystopper who inappropriately consents to a child's behavior, a pathologic relationship develops that leads to serious health, social and mental repercussions for the child and the parents. Ultimately it will severely damage the marriage.

Over the last few years, I have seen an alarming increase of divorce and have witnessed firsthand the dysfunctional emotional, mental and physical consequences it has on children. It is hard to believe but many parents get divorced because of Crystopper behavior. Ironically, divorce only makes Crystopper behavior worse.

Inevitably, it is the children who end up in the middle of bitter fights among divorced parents. There are always arguments about the weekend assignments to watch the children, and former spouses tend to compete with one another, trying to buy their children's love. The end result is that divorced parents become the worst Crystoppers, creating an opening for their children to manipulate not only their parents, but all the adults in their lives.

THREE AREAS REQUIRING TOTAL PARENTAL CONTROL

There are three spheres of control that parents must conquer in order to successfully raise their children. These spheres apply from birth and continue all the way through high school. I will discuss how to deal with the three areas with regards to different age groups in the following chapters.

SPHERE 1: NOCTURNAL SLEEPING

Parents should be capable of teaching their children to have an independent, uninterrupted night sleep. Babies should begin to do this in the first few months of their lives. Babies and toddlers should not be roaming around after 8 or 9 p.m. It is distressing to see numerous children and toddlers, and their exhausted, sleep-deprived parents that have not slept through the night since their child's infancy. This is not at all the children's fault; the fault lies with the Crystopper parents.

It is heartbreaking to see children that are not capable of sleeping in their own room for the entire night.

Many children don't have scheduled sleeping habits and fail to go to bed easily. These children are whiny, moody, temperamental, disobedient, misbehaved, disrespectful and even physically aggressive.

As a consequence, sleep problems could continue through adolescence, seriously affecting performance in school, energy levels and athletic abilities.

Moreover, when parents are unable to have a restful night, they lack the ability to have private time as a couple, causing tension that may lead to troubled marriages. Additionally, a parent who has not slept is less-equipped to deal with her children during the day, and will, as a result, make poor decisions regarding her child's health and well-being.

SPHERE 2: BEHAVIORAL & TEMPERAMENTAL

This is an area that parents find very difficult to control. In order to succeed, you have to believe and be convinced that your children are intelligent and capable of manipulation since the first few days of their lives.

From the first few days of a baby's life, parents realize the child has the ability to control them completely. When a baby is happy and relaxed in the parent's arms, and then cries immediately the second he is put down and stops as soon as he is picked up, it's clear he has learned quite a bit.

The baby has already discovered that crying will get the results he wants and that parents will hold him for a very long time just to avoid hearing him cry. Later on, he will probably learn that whining and temper tantrums achieve the same result.

These behavioral problems continue into adolescence, turning an undisciplined child into a troubled teenager. I have seen many cases where the police were required to intervene in order to discipline a young adult.

These are the children we see in restaurants, planes, supermarkets and cinemas who scream, throw temper tantrums and are basically out of control. As incredible as it sounds, this is a problem in more than 90% of households. Again, this is not the fault of the children, but the responsibility of the parents who allowed and continue to allow this type of behavior. This is the result of Crystopping.

SPHERE 3: NUTRITIONAL

There is a national epidemic of childhood obesity and poor eating habits. It is not rare to see 5 year old children who are 30-40 lbs. overweight. The majority of children acquire 95% of their daily caloric intake from carbohydrates, i.e. sugars. This unhealthy diet leads to serious medical problems, both during early childhood, teenage years and adulthood, with the potential of shortening a life span by as much as 5-15 years.

Over the last few years I have seen a significant number of children and teenagers with Diabetes Type II; also known as Adult Onset Diabetes. This condition is caused by obesity.

Every wellness check-up, and even during regular office visits, I try to convince parents how crucial it is to establish a healthy lifestyle during the first few years of life. Unfortunately, very often I notice children that are significantly overweight as early as 2-5 years of age.

Obviously most parents agree with me that unhealthy eating habits have serious consequences for their child's well-being. They also agree that if the family's lifestyle does not change, the child could develop obesity diabetes, high blood pressure, stroke, etc.

However, as soon as they go back home their Crystopper instinct takes over. Very soon they forget their commitment to change their lifestyles at home. They believe in a healthful life, but are unable to commit to leading one and the consequence is that their child develops serious health issues.

Besides affecting children's health and longevity, an unhealthy lifestyle may also inhibit a child's growth, preventing them from reaching their genetic height.

Short stature could cause psychological problems, and diminish their self-esteem.

This very dangerous trend is also 100% the fault of parents.

Children that grow up to become unhealthy adults as a result of an inappropriate lifestyle during their upbringing will frequently confront and accuse their parents of being responsible for their poor health and for a potential premature death.

VACCINATIONS

Originally I was not going to discuss vaccinations in this parenting guide. However, over the last decade I have learned that far too often enough parents make decisions regarding immunizations for their children based on unreliable advice from family and friends, or from the internet.

In the beginning of the book I mentioned that the basic rules of parenting are:

1) If something is bad for your child, DO NOT DO IT.
2) If something is good for your child, DO IT.

Vaccinations belong to the basic rule: IF IT IS GOOD FOR YOUR CHILD, DO IT.

As you know, many deadly diseases have been eradicated from the world, such as smallpox and polio, by the introduction of vaccines.

However, measles, a disease that almost vanished from the western hemisphere, has come back with a vengeance. Why? Over the last decade, parents have believed a false charge, spread by a British physician, that the measles vaccine could lead to autism. His statements regarding the link between the measles vaccine and autism have been proven groundless and many international studies have shown this theory to completely false. As a result, and the damage it has done to millions of children worldwide, the doctor has been discredited and his medical license has been revoked.

Alarmingly, the decline in measles vaccinations has led to unnecessary deaths and many more wild measles virus infections, causing children to suffer brain damage.

Trust your pediatrician when you are advised about vaccines; failure to immunize your child is like playing Russian roulette with your child's life.

During the early 1980's, I was doing a check up on a 2-month-old baby. When I completed my examination I told the mother that the baby needed the vaccinations required for that age. To my surprise, the mother refused based on the advice of her brother, a chiropractor. She said he told her that vaccines in the USA were part of a government "conspiracy" to inoculate children with toxic, experimental products.

I tried to educate her again at the following check-up. Despite my best efforts, I was unable to convince her. Eventually she got upset by my insistence and changed to another pediatrician more receptive to her point of view. A few months later I learned her son was diagnosed with a bacterial brain infection that would have been 100% preventable if she would have agreed to give her son that vaccine. Her son survived, but as a consequence became mentally challenged and partially deaf.

In my pediatric practice we do not accept patients who are not immunized. Vaccinations prevent many of the most deadly viral and bacterial infections. As a pediatrician, when I am on call, I often get after hours urgent calls from parents of a child with fever or other unusual symptoms. It is reassuring to know that these children were properly immunized. Otherwise, the child's life could be in great danger.

There are many things in life that we cannot control, such as a natural disaster or a car accident. However, if a child dies from a vaccine preventable disease, it is the biggest, saddest tragedy. That is why I refuse to accept patients in my practice that are not properly vaccinated. I do not want to be the one signing the death certificate of such a child.

POSTPARTUM DEPRESSION/ANXIETY VS. CRYSTOPPING

Postpartum depression occurs in about 10% of women.

It is very important to separate the symptoms of postpartum depression from those of Crystopping parents.

Often this condition may present itself as anxiety. This means that the normal level of worrying that all new mothers experience will present itself as pathologic exaggerated worrying. These mothers will overreact in a very inflated way to any variation of normal concern. They will often cry for no reason.

If you are not sure how to differentiate between normal, new mother apprehension and pathologic anxiety or depression, please consult with your personal physician ASAP. Remember: if you don't treat this condition it could lead to serious harm to the child and the mother.

DISCLAIMER

The purpose of this guide is to help you become successful parents, and to raise healthy, well balanced children and teenagers, both physical and emotional.

The final decision regarding the implementation of the guidelines in this handbook should be between you and your health care provider.

Chapter II

IS YOUR BABY INTELLIGENT AND CAPABLE FROM BIRTH?

A few years ago a patient showed me an article she found in a magazine. The article, written by a psychologist, was entitled, "There is No Such Thing as Spoiling a Child Under Six Months of Age."

The article postulated the flawed theory that a child less than six months old should always be appeased when he cried, but after six months it would be acceptable to allow a child to cry.

I was shocked by the article. On what basis did this psychologist determine that 6 months was the cut-off point? Does a child become more intelligent or emotionally independent at 6 months?

When I questioned this psychologist about the scientific methodology he used to determine the appropriate age for allowing babies to cry, he had no answer. He said that it just did not feel right to let a young baby cry.

Our planet hosts thousands of species, with human beings at the top of the evolutionary ladder. In fact, we know that other, less intelligent mammals can be taught, whether by their parents or trainers, to do a number of different complicated tasks from the very first weeks of life. And yet we don't expect the same abilities from our children. Often, I see young infants that cry every time they are left alone or put down for a nap. Many children maintain very erratic eating schedules.

At the same time, these same families will own pets that are so well-conditioned that they follow directions to sit, jump or stop barking. It seems to be that, sadly, parents have more faith in their pet's capabilities than in their children's. In fact, a former professor of mine told me that children are hard workers from birth.

They wake up in the morning with the goal of seeing how much information or knowledge they can learn from the people that surround them, i.e. parents, grandparents, and baby sitters. In order to get what they want, they "sell merchandise" in the form of crying, screaming, whining, throwing temper tantrums, even hugging and kissing. This type of "merchandise" has the ability to blind parental common sense and even basic logic. It is the parent who must dictate the child's behavior, not the other way around.

Chapter III

HOW ARE YOU PERCEIVED BY YOUR BABY?

To understand how our children perceive us, all we need to do is to reflect on our attitude as young adults in college or graduate school, meeting our new teachers on the first day of school.

If a teacher shows up late, fails to control the class, or gives students passing grades regardless of whether or not they put effort into their work, the teacher tends to be taken advantage of by the students. The teacher is not demanding that the students respect him or his authority, and the students therefore do not. Those students who do not resent the teacher for shortchanging them on their education may feel they like the teacher, but the teacher's job is not to be liked but to be learned from.

Alternatively, a teacher who establishes control and discipline, demands attention to assignments and gives grades that reflect the students' efforts and accomplishments may or may not be well-liked, and in fact may be considered overly strict or demanding, but will certainly be respected as a successful teacher. The students, even if they are resistant at first, will eventually gain from such a teacher and therefore have a feeling of accomplishment and self-satisfaction.

A few years ago I read about a study conducted on a college campus that dealt with the ability to be a good parent. The students in the study were not part of any psychology course. They were given a series of multiple choice questions regarding common issues i.e., how to teach a baby to sleep all night, how to prevent picky eating habits, how to respond to temper tantrums, how to control and prevent violent behavior, etc.

The majority of participating students answered most questions correctly. A few years later, many of them became parents, and not surprisingly, the way they behaved with their own children was exactly the opposite of the answers they had given.

We can deduce from this that even parents who intellectually know what they should do still do not act on that knowledge. Somehow, when faced with an actual child, parents forget all of their good intentions and rational thinking.

One of the biggest obstacles challenging young adults from parenting correctly is the idea that babies and young children are not capable of intelligent, pre-meditated behavior.

In a study conducted a few years ago, it was proven that a baby can recognize his mother since the first few weeks of life. Also, a child that is only few weeks old will cry hysterically to get the mother's attention, but will immediately stop crying once he is picked up.

The human brain, especially the brain of a newborn, deserves more credit than we attribute to it.

If parents learn to value and understand children's intelligence and capabilities from birth, they will begin to expect more from their children and, with the proper reinforcement, their children will expect more from themselves.

Chapter IV

PARENTAL ABUSE

One of the most horrible crimes that afflict our society is child abuse, meaning parents or caretakers that physically and/or emotionally abuse children.

However, very few people are aware that for each child victim of abuse, there are millions of parents and caretakers that are mentally and physically abused by the children they take care of.

Crystopper parents are totally exhausted, completely unable to function because their otherwise healthy toddler hasn't slept through the night since infancy. These parents walk in and out of the child's room numerous times during the night to respond to constant crying.

How often do we see toddlers and even school age children hitting, slapping, pinching, throwing objects and screaming profanities at their parents? This occurs frequently in public places like shopping malls, restaurants, airplanes or supermarkets. The sight of children screaming or throwing a temper tantrum is most often accompanied by the sight of bewildered parents who don't know how to control them.

A few years ago, I was examining two siblings with asthma, ages 5 and 3 years old. As the children's mother was trying to listen to my medical instructions, the five year old began to demand her attention. The mother asked him to wait. The child got upset and proceeded to punch her several times in the stomach and back. Her response was, "Sweetie, don't swing your arms that way, you may hurt Mommy."

One of the most traumatic cases of parental abuse I saw as a pediatrician began with a phone call from a very nervous and anxious father. I was paged because his first grader was physically attacking him and his wife. He would repeatedly curse, hit them, and throw objects at them.

As I was talking to the father I heard loud noises in the background— the sounds of breaking glass and screaming. I was so concerned that I felt that it was necessary to see the child in the emergency room to rule out abnormal behavior due to intoxication or a physical ailment.

In the emergency room I met a very normal looking child who was respectful, well-behaved and did not show signs of any physical or neurological abnormalities. All laboratory tests were normal.

The parents were highly educated people. The father was a professional builder who owned a construction company where he supervised hundreds of employees. The mother was a high school teacher. They told me that the child was always stubborn and strong-willed. They said that he entered into the "terrible twos" at nine months of age. Oddly, they claimed that he was doing well in school, and that they never got a call regarding any behavioral problems.

The following day I called the school teacher. She told me that this particular child was her best student. She described him as polite, respectful and a role model to other students.

The question that immediately came to mind was: are we talking about the same child? In fact, we were, but what I learned from speaking with the teacher and the parents is that while the child is the same, the adults are not. His school teacher was a very experienced professional. She was very strict, able to control and teach 25 students in one classroom. She had no time for "monkey business." On the first day of school she let the students know that misbehavior would not be tolerated. She did not make false threats.

This particular child was initially intimidated and scared when he met her. A few weeks later he determined that she was "awesome." He began to admire her, and became the classroom helper. He did everything possible to please her. He even helped discipline other children. He saw in this teacher a role model; he said he wanted to be like her when he got older.

Anytime that he began to do something wrong in school, just a simple look from the teacher would make him stop. She achieved a perfect balance. On the one hand, the child admired her, but on the other hand he knew that when she said "stop," he had to stop.

This is the perfect relationship between student and teacher. The student loves the teacher because he respects her authority. He enjoys his time with her because he has a clear understanding of the boundaries of their relationship.

His parents, however, were very different. Over the years he learned to view them as "objects" that were there to "serve" him. He had no respect for his parents, nor did he look up to them with admiration. He actually looked down at them as they were servants and maids. By then he knew how to squeeze everything he wanted from them. They had not established their authority over him, and he therefore did not respect them or acknowledge them as authorities.

After a few meetings, the parents of this child learned how to stop being Crystoppers. It was more difficult at this child's age, but by immediately changing the way they reacted to the child, demanding respect and instilling their authority in all how the child behaves, they were able to finally become true parents.

If parents allow their children to continually abuse them mentally and emotionally when they are young, they risk being physically abused once their children become teen-agers at which point they are strong enough to cause serious damage.

This was unfortunately the case a few years ago when a teenage boy physically attacked his mother. She ended up in the hospital with many broken bones. Her son went to juvenile detention. It is very important to realize that if we act as slaves and servants to our children we will never earn their respect, but above all we will never earn their love.

Chapter V

CRYSTOPPING PREVENTION GUIDE BY AGES

FIRST WEEK-SIX MONTHS

SPHERE 1: SLEEPING

Getting a child to sleep through the night is one of the most difficult hurdles facing new parents. A child who wakes repeatedly and needs to be fed or comforted to fall back to sleep can be disastrous for a parent's psychological, emotional and physical health. As you will read, there are many factors, including feeding and crib time routines that affect your child's ability to sleep well at night.

The best approach to a good night's sleep has 3 steps:

First: finish a full feeding

Second: change the baby into a clean diaper

Third: put the baby in his crib fully awake, sing a song, and then leave the room (it is ok to play easy listening or classic music near the crib).

Sadly, most parents don't follow the three-step routine. Instead they practice the dancing routine. Most parents know how to feed and change their baby but will allow the child to fall asleep while eating, or will proceed to dance and rock the baby until it falls asleep. Moreover, the dance will continue throughout the night, every time the baby wakes up.

Some parents will even take the baby out in the middle of the night for a stroller or car ride to get him to fall back to sleep.

While this seems to be a good solution in the short term—the baby does eventually go to sleep—in the long term, you are preventing the baby from learning the skill of going to sleep on his own. Therefore, and for many years to come, parents are sleep-deprived, cranky and miserable, a slave to their children's middle of the night tantrums.

SPHERE 2: BEHAVIORAL

SHOULD YOU USE A PACIFIER?

Pacifiers are the source of a great deal of debate amongst parents. The reality is that babies do not really need a pacifier but parents often provide one because it makes their baby stop crying. This is based on the false notion that parents should never let their baby cry. The baby does not need it. It is the parent that thinks that the baby needs it.

That is part of the Crystopper philosophy: do not allow the baby to cry under any circumstance. I am not implying that you should ignore your baby's cry, but there are different types of cries. In many cases, the baby needs to learn to soothe herself without artificial intervention.

(Only one very limited study published in 2004-05, states that it's possible that when a pacifier is used ONLY at bed time, and NOT BEFORE two months, and for only a few minutes, it potentially could decrease the incidence of crib death. This information should be discussed with your health care provider.)

In addition to being unnecessary, pacifiers are associated with an increased rate of ear and gastrointestinal infections. They are implicated in breast feeding interference and unwashed pacifiers, which are common as children will often pick up a pacifier from the floor and put it in their mouth without washing it, can cause an assortment of bacteria to enter the body.

Using a pacifier also affects a baby's, and therefore a parent's, nighttime routine. Whenever the pacifier falls out of the baby's mouth, the parent is awakened to retrieve it and then somehow get the child to fall back to sleep.

SPHERE 3: NUTRITIONAL

FEEDINGS

For a new mother, modern times can be very confusing. There are many conflicting methods on how to breast or bottle feed a baby. Even though there could be small variations, there are basically two methods:

1) ON DEMAND

This method calls for a mother to breast feed her baby anytime the baby cries, for as long as the baby wants. This means that if the baby decides to feed 20 times daily for an hour each time, the poor mother has to go along with it.

Instead of true breast feeding, some babies Snack Feed. For example, a baby nurses for seven minutes on the right side and then falls asleep, despite all efforts to awaken him. Within the hour, the baby wakes up from hunger, nurses five minutes, and goes back to sleep.

This scenario repeats itself over and over, sometimes with the baby falling asleep still latched on to the mother's breast, leaving the mother unable to move for the duration of the nap. Parents need to understand that it takes approximately 3 hours for a baby's full stomach to be empty. Feeding the baby within 1 or 2 hours will create a situation in which the stomach has breast milk in different stages of digestion, making it more likely for the baby to suffer from indigestion.

If the baby has indigestion, he will have gas pain. He will then cry louder. The mother will think that the baby is crying because of hunger, therefore she will continue an overfeeding cycle, teaching the baby that eating is the solution to any type of discomfort and eventually making the baby and the parents miserable.

2) SCHEDULED FEEDINGS

This method applies only to full term, healthy newborn babies.

Based on the fact that it takes an average of 3 hours for a full stomach to empty, it is more appropriate, from a physiological standpoint, to establish a schedule from the first few days of life. When beginning a scheduled breast feeding routine, it is very helpful to document the time when nursing begins, and on which side the feeding began (right or left breast). It is advisable to ask the gynecologist or a nurse to check the breast feeding mother for any nipple abnormalities that may make breast feeding more difficult, such as inverted nipples. Mothers with abnormalities will be advised on how to help their baby adapt so that they can breast feed successfully.

For mothers adopting a scheduled feeding routine, it is advisable to limit the baby's feeding time to 10-12 minutes on each breast. Why? A healthy, strong baby can ingest the breast milk that contains the highest concentration of nutrients in approximately the first 10 minutes of nursing. Allowing the baby to nurse for longer periods of time will mean that she is probably nursing on dry. This allows the baby's saliva to remain on the nipple for an excessive amount of time, resulting in painful, bleeding nipple fissures (see below for more information on this topic).

Again, it is advisable to limit nursing to no more than 10-12 minutes on each side. It is also important to burp the baby between sides. Wait a minimum of two and a half hours from the time you have finished feeding the baby before beginning the next feeding.

A WORD ABOUT BLEEDING NIPPLE FISSURES

Often I see parents get the scare of their lives when their otherwise healthy, breast feeding baby suddenly vomits blood. Their immediate reaction is to call 911 and rush to the hospital.

In the great majority of cases, the mother has bleeding fissures. Frequently, fissures are painless; therefore the mother is unaware she has them.

Recently I saw a 2 month old baby that came to the office because the baby was vomiting blood, but was otherwise symptom free. This case was unique because this mother had many other children and a lot of experience with breast feeding.

When I told her that most likely she had nipple fissures she denied it because she had checked herself before. On my insistence she visited her gynecologist who found two hidden fissures.

The only way that you can prevent nipple fissures is by removing the baby's saliva from your skin IMMEDIATELY after finishing nursing on one side. A clean, wet cloth will be enough, followed by some lanolin cream.

Only after you have taken care of yourself, go to the other breast

BREAST FEEDING STARVATION

Another reason for limiting the length of breast feeding time is to prevent an infrequent but dangerous condition called breast feeding starvation. This is a condition in which the breast feeding mother does not have enough milk, but she keeps on nursing. The baby begins to lose weight, and in some cases it could lead to severe malnutrition and failure to thrive.

In our practice, we have seen many cases of breast-fed starved babies. The most severe case happened in early 2006. This first-time mother was very confused on whose advice to follow. She had come to a prenatal meeting but was not very convinced of the appropriateness of my "feeding on a schedule" method because she had met with two lactation consultants who had convinced her that "feeding on demand" was the most appropriate.

Therefore, she breast fed approximately every hour on the hour. We saw the baby when he was 14 days old. He had lost about 10% of his birth weight, but it is not uncommon for breast fed babies to lose weight during the first two weeks.

Nevertheless, I was concerned about the frequent feedings and the fact that at two weeks the baby had not recovered his birth weight. I suggested to the mother that she limit the breast feeding time to a maximum of 12 minutes on each side, and if the baby was still hungry she was to immediately supplement with formula. She was told to return in five to seven days to re-weigh the baby.

She did not follow that advice because her lactation consultant assured her that "cluster feeding" would solve the problem. She brought the baby to the office again at seven weeks of age with a fever of 102 degrees and a weight of six pounds, two pounds less than his birth weight. The baby was hospitalized, recovered his weight, and eventually continued breast feeding on a schedule, but with a formula supplement.

After 10-12 minutes on each breast, a baby who is still "acting hungry," should receive a supplementary bottle feeding.

Most importantly, if at any time you become concerned for your child's health or well-being, you must consult with a medical professional. Recently I consulted with a couple who, even though they live 30 miles from my office, came to see me because they were desperately trying to create a scheduled feeding system for a baby that was crying day and night.

Before giving any advice, I requested to examine the baby. As it turned out, the baby was suffering from a condition called GERD (gastro esophageal reflux). Once that condition was controlled, the baby improved dramatically.

Therefore you must always have your health care provider examine your baby and follow his or her advice.

Unfortunately, there is a widespread misconception that if a baby who is successfully breast feeding gets "exposed" to bottle feeding, she will develop **"nipple confusion"** and "never" be able to nurse again.

My experience and evolutional studies have shown that a newborn baby is an intelligent human being from birth, capable of differentiating between different options and often choosing the "easy way out."

When a baby realizes that bottle feeding is easier and requires less effort than breastfeeding, they may try to persuade their mother to stop breast feeding and switch to bottle feeding.

Those that believe in nipple confusion forget that all living beings, including newborns, have a strong survival instinct. This means that when you are really, really hungry, you will eat whatever it is no matter where it comes from.

It is not difficult to cure nipple confusion in a baby that was previously breast feeding fine but now strictly prefers the bottle. For example, if it is seven o'clock in the morning and the baby refuses to nurse, stop trying. Do not bottle feed. Wait one hour, then try breast feeding again. If the baby refuses again, you can be certain that after a few hours it will be so hungry that it will happily take sustenance in any form it is offered. To be successful in curing nipple confusion, parents must understand that it is not so terrible to let a baby cry for a few hours.

They must realize that wise parents only have the well-being of their child in mind, regardless of crying. Unfortunately, Crystopper parents will succumb after a few minutes of crying and will give the baby a bottle, at which point the baby loses the benefit of breastfeeding because the parents were not diligent enough in their efforts.

WAKING UP THE BABY FOR FEEDING PURPOSES

Healthy, full-term babies will initially feed every 3-4 hours. As previously mentioned, do not feed the baby before 3-4 hours from finishing time. However, if your baby wants to be fed less frequently, i.e. 4-5 hours, and weight gain is appropriate, it would be an insult to your baby's intelligence to wake her up.

The only exception is if there is confusion between day and night. In such cases the baby may sleep from noon to 6 p.m., and then stay awake for 3-4 hours during the night. Obviously it is preferable for the baby to sleep for 6 hours but from midnight to 6 a.m. This could very easily be achieved by following the recommendations found in the next chapter, "Scheduled Feeding and Sleeping Through The Night."

BOTTLE USE IN BREAST FED BABIES—
AND FATHER'S PARTICIPATION

Even the most successful scheduled breast feeding mother needs a break. Even if the baby is on a four hour feeding routine, it is unfair to enslave a mother by creating a situation where she is the only person in the world that can feed the baby. Mothers have other commitments, whether it's other children, professional responsibilities or household necessities. It is also important for the father to be actively involved.

Therefore, it is beneficial to teach the baby from the first week of life to accept feedings from both the breast and the bottle. It may be a good idea to start a routine such that before the last late evening feeding the baby gets a full bath (assuming the umbilical cord is already fallen) and then breast milk in a bottle given by the father. This kind of routine helps the baby develop the notion of a day/night cycle.

Breast milk could be stored for months in the freezer and for approximately 72 hours in the refrigerator. Once a baby is fully conditioned to take either breast or bottle without any struggle, it will be smooth sailing until the child is introduced to solid food at approximately at six months of age.

Getting a baby used to taking a bottle is beneficial for other reasons as well. It is commonly known that, difficult as it may be for a parent to separate from a baby, it is good for the parents and their relationship to escape from their daily routine and spend some quality time together.

If a couple is blessed to have family members that are reliable babysitters, once the baby is over two or three months old, parents could take a bit of a vacation. During this time their baby would still get breast milk (that was stored in the freezer in advance) from the bottle.

Dietary restrictions imposed on some mothers because of their child's sensitivity could be a burden. However, it does not have to mean that the mother remain limited indefinitely. On an occasion when she would like to indulge in otherwise restricted food, she would merely need to pump breast milk in advance and give the stored milk to the baby for the 12 hours following. Milk pumped during the 12 hours after she ate the restricted food would be discarded.

In summary, teaching the baby to take breast milk either directly from the mother or from a bottle would facilitate the goal of breast feeding for the advised twelve months. By approaching the issue logically and considering the importance of safeguarding both the child's and the mother's physical and psychological health and well-being, breastfeeding can be an enjoyable and easy experience for mother and child.

FORMULA FEEDING

While it is widely acknowledged that breast feeding provides the best nutrition for newborn babies, there are some parents who, for a variety of reasons, choose to bottle feed formula.

CHOOSING THE RIGHT FORMULA

It is crucial to consult with your pediatrician regarding the formula that best fulfills your baby's needs. There are many brands of baby formula. Most of them consist of either milk-based, soy-based, lactose free or hydrolyzed protein. Inform your pediatrician about any family history of milk allergies, or allergic conditions such as asthma, hay fever or eczema.

SCHEDULED BOTTLE FEEDING

This method is applicable only for healthy, full term babies.

Based on the fact that it takes an average of three hours for a baby's stomach to empty itself, it is very important to follow a strict schedule.

There are only two basic rules:

1) Do not bottle feed for more than 20 minutes but do not limit the quantity your child ingests in that time period. These time frames do not include burping time. Practically, it should not take more than 30 minutes from start to finish.
2) Do not feed the baby again for a minimum of 3 to 4 hours from finishing time.

Feeding the baby for more than 20 minutes or more than once within 3 to 4 hours can cause vomiting, stomach pain, indigestion and sometimes abnormal bowel movements. Overfeeding could also lead to unnecessary weight gain. Very often I take care of new patients that have been diagnosed with colic, reflux, and milk intolerance whose symptoms disappear once a feeding schedule is introduced.

IS YOUR NIGHT YOUR BABY'S NIGHT TOO?

There is a very important relationship between scheduled day time feeding and a baby's ability to develop appropriate night time sleep. You know that your baby is ready to establish night sleep when he is capable of sleeping for a larger period of time, at least 5-8 hours.

Unfortunately, your baby's night may not coincide with your own. It is not enough for a baby to sleep 5-8 hours—they must be the correct 5-8 hours. It is not beneficial for a baby to sleep between 2 p.m. to 8 p.m. If he exhibited the ability to sleep 5-8 hours, we have to make sure that it correlates with the parents' night cycle, i.e. midnight to 5 or 6 a.m. (It is not beneficial for the baby or the family if the baby sleeps from 2 p.m. to 8 p.m., nor from 9 p.m. to 3 a.m.)

To teach a baby to sleep a full, uninterrupted night, all that it is necessary is conditioned behavior.

LAST FEEDING OF THE DAY AND SLEEPING THROUGHOUT THE NIGHT

As previously discussed, regardless of whether the baby is nursing or bottle feeding, the last feeding of the day, typically the one between 10 p.m. and midnight, should be from a bottle of breast milk or formula.

The baby should be given a bath, a bottle feeding (ideally by the father), and bed time in a crib in a quiet, private room. In order to be successful, it is essential to follow the following recommendations:

1) Finish the late afternoon feeding at least 4-5 hours prior to the last feeding (somewhere between 6-7 p.m.).
2) After the late afternoon feeding, do not allow the baby to fall into a deep sleep.
3) Give the baby a long bath prior to the last feeding (approximately between 10-11:30 p.m.). Take your time to apply baby

moisturizing cream, and change the diaper and then provide the last feeding.

It is important to follow these steps because during the interval between the last late afternoon feeding, and the last feeding of the day, the baby should not be allowed to fall into a deep sleep as that may prevent the baby from doing so later.

A long warm bath will increase the baby's appetite and allow the baby to consume a larger volume of fluid, thereby preparing him or her for a long, uninterrupted sleep.

The ingestion of a larger amount of breast milk/formula, the fatigue, a firm crib mattress and a quiet, dark, private environment will soon teach the baby to have an uninterrupted night's sleep.

MULTIPLE BIRTHS

Parenting is probably one of the most difficult, and at the same time most rewarding, jobs in the world, even when raising more than one child at a time. Over the last two decades, the number of multiple births has dramatically increased, probably in part due to the increased use of fertility drugs.

Raising multiple children is a challenge. Being a Crystopper instead of a parent creates serious challenges when there are multiple births, and it creates a nightmare for the entire family.

As mentioned before, all babies must:

A) Be totally healthy, and full term weight (always check with your pediatrician first).
B) Have achieved a gestational age of 38-40 weeks, and/or a weight of seven pounds.
C) Acquire the skill of nursing and/or bottle feeding or both.

To be successful when caring for multiple babies, you must apply similar principles as those suggested for one baby. However there are a few differences.

COMBINED BREAST AND BOTTLE FEEDING MULTIPLE BABIES

Many mothers can partially breast feed multiple babies. Some lactation consultants claim that a mother can hold and simultaneously feed two babies.

It is my personal view that simultaneous breast feeding is a very difficult and technically complicated task. You may try it if you want but it is more practical to combine bottle and breast feeding.

In order to be successful when it comes to feeding more than one baby, you must:

1) Make sure that you have enough breast milk to provide the required nutrients for each baby. Follow the guidelines mentioned in the beginning of the chapter regarding breast and bottle feedings, and ensure that all your babies meet the health, weight and maturity criteria.

2) As recommended before, follow the same guidelines regarding frequency, feeding time and quantity.

3) Follow the feeding schedule of the baby that sleeps the longest.

For example, if baby A feeds every four hours, but baby B wants to eat after three hours and fifteen minutes, you should wait until baby A wakes up, and then try to feed them simultaneously. It is easier if you are blessed to have help at home, especially when you are combining breast and formula feeding.

Try to keep an accurate record of each feeding in order to remember the time when you finished their feeding, and which baby was breast or bottle fed.

If you have no help, try to feed them at the same time to the extent possible.

BOTTLE FEEDING MULTIPLE BABIES

If you are exclusively bottle feeding, it is possible to do simultaneous feedings even if you do not have help. You can use car seats to keep all babies securely fastened in the appropriate position, and then carefully feed them. You must be very familiar with the car seats safety features in case you need to take care of a baby that is vomiting, chocking or having any kind of trouble.

Be aware that it is completely acceptable to make the baby that woke up first wait until the other baby wakes up to begin feeding. It will probably take a few days for all babies to be on the same schedule.

I have a patient who had triplet boys many years ago. She followed my advice about the right way to feed multiple babies and was so successful that she created a support group to help other parents with multiple babies.

FEEDING AND SLEEPING BEYOND THE FIRST TWO WEEKS

If you follow the advice previously given, you will see that the majority of healthy babies begin to develop a more defined pattern of feedings and sleep by two weeks of age.

As mentioned above, besides feeding in a scheduled, predictable way, a night pattern begins to develop. Soon you will notice a period of time during which the baby will sleep uninterrupted 5-7 hours and will eat during the day in approximately a four hour cycle.

Don't forget that you must make sure that your night is the baby's night too. Follow the steps mentioned before in, "IS YOUR NIGHT YOUR BABY'S NIGHT TOO?"

Once you have achieved a consistent pattern of night sleeping (approximately 11 p.m. to 5 or 6 a.m.), you have to progressively add more sleep time by backing up previous feedings. For example, if the last late afternoon feeding is completed by 7 p.m., and the last feeding of the night is completed by midnight, (you have to give the baby a bath prior to the last feeding), then you back up the 7 p.m. feeding to 6:30 p.m., (you do the same with the previous feedings too), then make it so that you finish the last feeding of the night by 11:30 p.m., and do not feed the baby again until 5 or 6 a.m.

Your goal should be that by two months of age, your baby should have an uninterrupted sleep of at least 8 hours and by four to six months the baby should sleep uninterrupted for 10-12 hours.

IMPORTANT 'DO NOT DOS'

Once you put the baby in the crib, DO NOT walk in and out the room. It is preferable for you to purchase an audio/ video monitor with night vision, so you can watch and observe the baby for as long as you want. That way you can see if something is wrong. If the baby learns that crying will bring a parent into the room, the baby will not be able to sleep well.

There are always excuses to go into the baby's room. Please be strong. Do not go in to put back the pacifier, adjust the temperature, or just peek in. The most important rule: *no room service!* Once the baby is in the crib, he stays in the crib until morning.

Within two to four nights the baby will learn to and enjoy sleeping all night, and you and your family will have a better quality of life, which, after all, will benefit the baby as well. As your baby gets older he will try to obtain night time room service again.

Typically, at approximately 6-9 months of age, and because of night time separation anxiety the baby may now have, the baby may wake up numerous times just to say, "Hello." When something like this happens, you may want to take the baby to the doctor just to make sure that the baby is healthy, and that there are no medical problems such as an ear infection, but otherwise, remain strong and remember that nighttime is for sleeping, not socializing.

Also you need to remember that if the baby was crying, and after being picked up stops crying within a few minutes, and begins crying when placed back into bed, there was nothing medically wrong with her. Once you learn that there are no medical problems you can continue taking the same approach, i.e. ignoring the episodes of night waking, and after a few nights the night time separation anxiety will fade.

Chapter VI

SIX TO TWELVE MONTHS OF AGE

SPHERE 1: SLEEP

At this stage, your baby should be able to sleep an uninterrupted 10-12 hours. Just remember the basic recommendations mentioned in the previous chapters.

- Make sure that the last nap of the day is completed by 4 p.m.
- Give the baby dinner at the same time as the rest of the family (approximately 6 p.m.)
- Give the baby a warm bath at approximately 8 p.m.

Previously I mentioned that formula should be given IMMEDIATELY after solid food. The only exception could be the last bottle of the day.

Give the baby dinner at the same time as everybody else in the family, but DO NOT GIVE A BOTTLE.

Right after bathing the baby, put her in a high chair and give her the last bottle or sippy cup of the day. Doing so will allow the baby to go to bed with a full stomach.

Change the baby's diaper, put him in the crib and do not provide any room service until the morning after.

Because of nighttime separation anxiety, your baby may wake up at night just to say hello.

Once you learn that every time you pick him up the crying stops almost immediately, you will realize that there is nothing physically wrong. (When in doubt, take the baby to the pediatrician to make sure that the baby is healthy.)

Then all you need to do is to teach the baby that even if he cries you are not going to intervene. You have to be strong and avoid any interaction with the baby during the night.

It is OK to watch the baby indirectly by using a video/audio monitor. Within a few nights, this night time separation anxiety will disappear.

SPHERE 2: BEHAVIORAL

SEPARATION ANXIETY

There are two kinds of separation anxiety:

A) Day Time

Your baby is fully convinced that your primary function in life is to be glued to her 24/7. At approximately 9 months of age, separation anxiety will reach its peak. However, it could start as early as six months or as late as 15.

To successfully gain control in the early stages, you have to program your day like a school teacher. For example, if your baby wakes up at 7 a.m., have breakfast, then set a time to play with her. Put her in the crib when it's time for a morning nap.

When the baby wakes up, put her in a designated safe play area such as a playpen. Some playpens have several attachments that makes them expandable and very safe for a baby (or even multiple babies).

Doing so will allow you to have time for yourself while your baby learns to spend some time alone. It is very important for a child to learn to entertain herself without being held. Obviously she will, at first, do everything possible to persuade you to pick her up by screaming and crying. Please do not give in.

B) NIGHT TIME

As discussed in the previous paragraphs, some babies who had been sleeping uninterrupted all night will suddenly awaken numerous times.

Once you verify that she is consolable within a few minutes and your pediatrician rules out any medical condition that could cause her to wake up, then it is perfectly acceptable to ignore the crying. Within a few nights the baby will get the message and separation anxiety will fade.

SAFETY

Once your baby learns to crawl, or is able to easily grab objects with both hands, safety becomes a major issue.

It is crucial to childproof the house. The American Academy of Pediatrics has guidelines on how to do so properly. Also there are many companies that specialize in childproofing your home.

Obviously you should remove any potential dangerous objects from the child's reach. Also you need to remove any hazardous chemicals from the bathroom and kitchen.

It is important to fence and secure any dangerous areas of the house like swimming pools, ovens and toilets. Learn how to lower the water heater's temperature to prevent third degree burns.

YOUR BABY IS READY FOR SOLID FOODS (SIX TO NINE MONTHS OF AGE)

The appropriate age to start solid food for your baby is six months, although in special circumstances there may be a need to start solid food earlier.

Studies have shown that introduction of solid food before six months could lead to food allergies. Some even suspect that the higher incidence of celiac disease (gluten intolerance) is related to early introduction of cereals.

BASIC RULES:

1) Food is edible and is intended for eating, not drinking

I often see patients insist on putting cereal in their baby's formula. Usually this is because someone has convinced them that it will help their baby sleep through the night, or that their baby is going through a growth spurt and needs the extra food.

That is not accurate. Healthy babies do not require any cereal in their formula. However, there are a few medical conditions that require the addition of cereal to the formula in order to thicken the liquid and either improve gastro-esophageal reflux, or to allow babies on fluid restriction to obtain more calories with a smaller fluid volume.

2) Solid food is given to the baby first, and then breast milk or formula.

Once your baby has finished the solid food part of the meal, immediately offer breast milk or formula. Do not wait even 5 minutes, because that will seem like a new meal.

3) Do not give the same food item twice the same day. For example, do not give cereal more than once daily.

4) Each new food item has to be tried for at least five consecutive days. If there are no side effects, or signs of intolerance, you may start a new item.

5) If the baby is allergic or intolerant of a specific food item, the most common symptoms are: vomiting, diarrhea, abdominal pain, and skin rashes. If you are unsure how to interpret any potential side effect, consult with your pediatrician. The doctor will tell you when it is safe to try that specific food item again.

6) During the first 12 months avoid exposing your baby to honey as it could lead to a very dangerous disease called botulism. Also avoid tropical fruits such as pineapple and mango. Some professionals recommend avoiding citrus and strawberries.

Consult with your pediatrician about when and how to expose your child to seafood, eggs and nuts. Avoid raw fish.

7) SOLID FOOD STAGES

The following recommendations apply only to healthy babies who do not suffer from any neurological condition that could interfere with the process of chewing and swallowing. When in doubt, consult your pediatrician.

Baby foods could be prepared with different levels of consistency.

Stage one is pureed food, which is considered table food, but is almost drinkable.

Stage two is more solid, and is made of a combination of different food items, like vegetables and poultry, cereal and fruits.

Stage three is very close to table food.

Table food: this kind of food is similar to regular table food, but it has to be made in such way that it is safe, and appropriate for a child that is still learning how to chew. Avoid round, hard food, such as peanuts and tree nuts, hot dogs and sausages (unless cut in very small pieces), raw, hard-to-chew vegetables (like raw carrots or celery) and hard-to-chew protein, like steak or very dry poultry.

Remember, the number of teeth a child has does not determine his ability to handle table food. There are many babies without a single tooth that are very coordinated and can handle table food. Some babies with many teeth, if they are not trained properly, are unable to chew any solid food.

8) WATER OR OTHER DRINKS

Sometime between 6-9 months of age, especially in warm climates, your baby may need water in between meals.

Please do NOT give fruit juices. Not even diluted ones. No matter which fruit it comes from, and regardless of how organic, or natural, or handmade it is, ultimately they are all only sugar.

Many patients become traumatized when I tell them that a diet drink is less detrimental to the child's health than fruit juice. If you give fruit juice to your baby, you will cause serious nutritional problems, like picky eating, short stature, and even carbohydrate dependence.

FOOD GROUPS

A) CEREALS

It is appropriate to start introducing this group with one cereal because, even though there is minimal nutrition value to them, when mixed with breast milk or formula the baby will recognize the flavor and will want to eat it immediately. If the baby is constipated, use oatmeal instead of rice cereal.

B) FRUITS

Begin with fruits like apple sauce, pear sauce, and ripe banana. Subsequently, you may add apricots, peaches, watermelon, cantaloupe, and many more.

C) YELLOW/ORANGE VEGETABLES

They are essential because they contain certain necessary vitamins, especially vitamin A, and should constitute 30% of your baby's total weekly vegetable servings. These include carrots, corn, squash and sweet potato.

D) GREEN VEGETABLES

Nutritionally speaking, green vegetables are crucial in order for your child to grow up healthy. Children who eat green vegetables grow up healthier and stronger. If you teach your child to eat green vegetables, you will decrease the risk of obesity and constipation.

Green vegetables should constitute 70% of your child's total weekly servings.

Unfortunately, it is almost impossible to find ready-made green vegetables in the baby food section, mainly because commercial baby food companies know that a baby quickly discovers that sweet potato tastes better than broccoli, and that corn tastes better than zucchini.

Therefore, it's a good idea to cook and freeze individual portions of zucchini, broccoli, chayote squash and cauliflower and then defrost them before mealtime.

E) PROTEINS: (from 6-9 months)

Once you have introduced your baby to the basic foods, i.e. cereal, fruits, yellow and green vegetables, you can start to introduce proteins. Start with poultry (chicken and turkey), then move on to meats (veal, lamb or beef). You can use the kind that baby food companies make, or make your own. If you choose to buy the ready-made brands, choose wisely.

Do not buy baby food that contains additives that your baby has never tried before. Additionally, stay away from protein loaded with starchy foods, such as pasta or rice.

HOW TO PREPARE PROTEIN

It is better if you personally select the best and freshest protein and boil it together with the recommended vegetables such as carrots, turnips, celery, onion and parsley. Do not be afraid to add salt and pepper as doing so will make the meat very soft and tender. Also, it will taste better and the better it tastes, the more likely your child will enjoy eating it.

Once the food is fully cooked, use a food processor to get it to a good consistency and store it in the freezer in single portions using individual containers or ice cube trays. You can then mix portions in any combination you prefer.

VEGETARIAN PROTEIN

For a variety of religious or personal reasons, many parents decide to restrict their children from eating animal protein. Some parents only restrict red meat from their children's diet, allowing protein-rich poultry, fish and eggs.

If you are planning to keep your baby away from all kinds of animal protein, consult with a pediatric nutritionist about how to use soy meat and other vegetarian products to ensure your baby gets the nutrients he needs to grow healthy and strong.

WATER SUPPLEMENTS

Between 6-9 months of age, some babies require water supplements, especially if he is outdoors a great deal. This is perfectly acceptable as long as you remember that your baby needs water, not sugar. Do not give fruit juices or electrolyte solutions. Do not give even "watered down" fruit juice. Believe it or not, diet sodas are LESS detrimental to your child's health than fruit juice.

SOLID FOOD AND YOUR BABY (NINE TO TWELVE MONTHS)

The following recommendations apply only to healthy babies that do not suffer from any neurological condition that could interfere with the process of chewing and swallowing. When in doubt, consult your pediatrician.

During the first few weeks of introducing solid food, baby food is made into puree, which is almost drinkable, and is made of only one food item. By nine months, the baby's ability to handle solid food should allow her to eat similar food items as the rest of the family.

NEW PROTEINS

By nine months, most babies have been introduced to poultry and meats like beef, veal and lamb. Unless there is a family history of allergies, or your pediatrician disagrees, you can also introduce eggs. Some suggest starting with scrambled yolk, and then giving the entire egg. Eggs are a great source of protein, and are versatile given that they can be cooked in so many ways. Even if there is a family history of elevated cholesterol, you can buy fat-free/cholesterol-free egg beaters and serve them as often as you like.

FISH

Between 9-12 months of age you may give your baby fish with the exception of crustaceous varieties such as shrimp, lobster, etc. Before doing so, discuss this issue with your pediatrician because of the possibility of food allergies.

Fish is a very delicate source of protein that must be bought fresh and served without bones. Additionally, canned tuna, prepared in water, is one of the safest sources of fish.

CHANGING FROM "WET" TO SOLID FOOD

Regardless of the number of teeth a baby has, you have to transition your baby's food from wet to dry. Create small, thread like pieces of chicken that are not completely dried, and mix them with similar-sized pieces of boiled zucchini or yellow or chayote squash. You can feed the baby or let him use his fingers.

MOTHER'S STASH OF ALL THE WRONG SNACKS

HEALTH HAZZARD WARNING: AVOID FRUIT JUICES AND OTHER UNHEALTHY, SUGAR-LOADED SNACKS

As previously mentioned, we are in the middle of an obesity epidemic. Even thin children have very poor eating habits.

Poor eating habits begin as early as approximately 9 months. As incredible as it sounds, 95% of parents carry the same stash in their diaper bag. This is usually some combination of fruit juice, cheerios, pretzels, dehydrated fruits, yogurts, animal cookies, saltines, raisins, rice crackers and granola.

Sadly, most parents think it is OK to give those snacks and are even proud, because they are influenced by propaganda such as *no sugar added, organic, vitamin supplemented fruit juice.* It is all a BIG LIE. ALL fruit juices are 100% CARBOHYDRATES which means 100% SUGAR.

Do not trick yourself into thinking that by watering down the juice you are doing something good. All you are doing is teaching your child that water on its own is not good enough and that it needs to be flavored. What is wrong with plain water?

Some parents think that if a drink is not sweet or flavored their baby will not drink it. Thinking that way is an insult to your baby. Nature is wise. When any mammal (cat or dog) is hungry or thirsty, it will eat or drink anything. Your baby is no different. When she is hungry or thirsty, she will eat or drink what she is given.

To complicate matters even more, by 9-12 months of age the honeymoon with food is over. It is human nature to prefer carbohydrates and a baby quickly learns that sweet potato, corn, pasta, rice, cookies tastes better than zucchini, broccoli and spinach.

That explains why when you try to buy baby food in the supermarket there are hundreds of choices for yellow vegetables and pasta, but very few, if any, choices of cooked green vegetables.

Obviously, there are tons of green vegetables that baby food companies could prepare. However, these companies know that 95% of parents are Crystoppers. They know that parents will give into their child's carbohydrate preferences. So they make what they know they can sell.

The combination of the mother's stash and the child's pickiness creates a scenario where by the time the baby turns 24 months old, 95% of his total caloric intake comes from carbohydrates.

CURING PICKINESS AND SELECTIVE EATING (from 9 to 15 months old)

It is human nature to prefer to eat carbohydrates instead of green vegetables and protein. As mentioned before, by 9 to 12 months of age a baby has tasted cereals, fruits, yellow and green vegetables, starchy food and protein.

Regardless of the order in which these foods were introduced between 9-to 12 months of age the baby will want, prefer and demand sweet, carbohydrate—loaded foods such as fruits, pasta, and sweet vegetables.

For example, let's say that you are giving your baby zucchini with chicken for lunch, and you know that in the past he ate that with delight. Suddenly, your baby refuses to eat and spits out his food. What should you do?

The majority of parents would enter into a state of panic. They will most likely assume that if they do not immediately provide an alternative the baby will be dangerously hungry and undernourished. But take this way of thinking one step further. Would you allow a 9 month old, or even an older child, to choose his menu? At that age, there wouldn't be one nutritious item on it!

SOLUTION: When the baby refuses to eat a HEALTHY meal (in this case zucchini with chicken), simply take him out of the chair. DO NOT provide any other food, or any formula. Wait 1 or 2 hours and then put the baby back on the high chair and offer the same food item again. Don't force-feed the baby. It is OK to give plain water in between.

Please be reassured that within a few hours the baby will eat ANYTHING you put in front of him. The teaching point here is that the instinct of survival is more powerful than any picky preferences. If your baby learns in the first 36 months of life that you are indifferent to their eating preferences, that all you care about is healthy eating habits, the struggle to have the child eat healthy food will be over very soon.

As mentioned before, inappropriate snacks could ruin any efforts to stop pickiness. Therefore, if you are in the process of teaching your baby that there are no alternatives to the menu, do not provide even healthy snacks—stick to meals.

Even if your baby is still in the honeymoon phase and eating all green vegetables and protein, avoid at all cost any of the popular baby snacks, such as fruit juices, cheerios, dehydrated fruits and fish cookies.

Once your baby learns that there are no alternatives to what you choose, and there are no more struggles, then it is ok to give snacks.

Snacks have to be based on cooked, green vegetables and water. I can assure you that your baby will enjoy the cooked zucchini, asparagus, green peas, cooked chayote squash, small pieces of chicken, cheeses, etc. as much as other babies enjoy their sugar filled snacks.

FINGER FOODS

Often when I ask parents to implement strict, health oriented, dietary control I am told that the only reason why they give cheerios to their children is for them to practice using their fingers for grabbing and pinching.

It is true that between 9-12 months babies need to learn how to grab food with their fingers. But contrary to popular belief, cheerios are not the only food a baby can grab. Give your baby small, cut, cooked squares of zucchini, carrots, asparagus or chayote. You can even offer canned green vegetables that are available in any supermarket and do not require a can opener such as asparagus, green peas, and hearts of palm (give only the soft parts cut in small pieces).

REMEMBER: if your child snacks on cereals, crackers and yogurts you are destroying her appetite for the meal to come. Even if you gave your baby two cans of green or low carbohydrate vegetables, her appetite for the next meal will be unaffected.

TABLE FOOD

BY nine months of age the average baby can be transitioned to safe, solid food, regardless of the presence of teeth. At nine months, it is possible, in most cases, to introduce eggs (scrambled) and fish, ideally canned tuna in water because it has no bones, and is unlikely to spoil. CONSULT WITH YOUR PEDIATRICIAN before starting eggs and fish.

Instead of chunky, wet, pureed foods, you can begin by taking boiled chicken, or meat, or fish and cut it in very small, string-like pieces. Instead of processing vegetables, cut them in very small pieces. You will be very pleased to see how much your baby enjoys this kind of food. You can begin to use a baby fork or try to find a fork without sharp ends. If your baby wants to help by using his hands, by all means let him.

FRUITS

You are going to transition from boiled or cooked pureed fruits to small pieces of real fresh fruits such as apple, pear, cantaloupe and watermelon. Continue to avoid the tropical fruits mentioned before.

Do not forget that your baby needs to have three servings of fruit daily, given **only after each meal**. However, try to choose low carbohydrate fruits. Minimize bananas and be very careful not to give raisins as they may cause choking.

Do not give fruits as snacks, before or in between meals. If you do so your baby's appetite for the following meal will be affected.

Chapter VII:

FIRST BIRTHDAY

First Birthday: 12-15 MONTHS

SPHERE 1: SLEEP

The rules for bedtime are similar to the ones established for babies between 6-12 months of age. However, in some cases, at this stage you could add a new routine: a bed time story.

Be aware that some children will not be interested in hearing a story until they get older, when their ability to comprehend improves. There are different books to choose from. Some can generate a variety of sounds when the parent or the child touches different pages; some are very colorful and have different textures.

Once you finish your story telling time, leave the room and do not provide room service of any kind until the following morning.

SPHERE 2: BEHAVIORAL

At this stage, your baby will begin to show signs of the "terrible twos." This exhibits itself as temper tantrums, whining and aggressive behavior. These will be discussed in greater detail in the next chapter, however two very important issues at this stage are THE BOTTLE AND THE PACIFIER.

BOTTLE AND PACIFIER AND HOW TO DISCONTINUE BOTH

PACIFIER

As previously mentioned, the baby NEVER NEEDED a pacifier. It was given by Crystopping parents that could not stand the crying, and therefore created an addiction for the baby that they now must break.

BOTTLE

The process of weaning the baby from the bottle begins at 9 months of age by instituting the use of spill proof cups.

Studies show that the most humane way for parents and their child to discontinue both bottle and pacifier is to remove them simultaneously. While many parents postpone doing this, it is cruel to wait until the baby is older and has become even more attached and therefore more aware when they are removed.

By 15 to 24 months, the child, now addicted to them, will begin to specifically request a bottle or pacifier. Bottle feeding beyond 12 months will actually damage the child's appetite, and create picky eating habits. Beyond 24 months, using a bottle or pacifier can lead to maxillofacial deformities.

SPHERE 3: NUTRITIONAL

The following items will be discussed again in the following chapter. You will notice some overlapping but similar advice between this stage and the over fifteen month's stage.

Once your baby celebrates her first birthday you can give your baby ANY TABLE FOOD ITEM, as long as you follow these basic guidelines:

A) Every new food item has to be tried for five consecutive days.

B) It has a consistency that the baby can handle, and it does not pose a choking hazard.

C) It has not been suspected as a cause for food allergies.

FIFTEEN-TWENTY FOUR MONTHS OF AGE

SPHERE 1: SLEEP

In the next chapter, I will discuss in more detail the sleeping needs for children older than two as well as the transition from crib to bed. However, at this stage the night time separation anxiety discussed in previous chapter may appear again.

Because many toddlers at this stage are beginning to use vocabulary, and are able to scream and cry and call their parents, things become a bit more complicated. On the one hand, now that the baby can communicate more effectively, it is easier for the parent to figure out what their child wants. On the other hand, when a mother hears, "Mommy, mommy, I love you, pick me up," she begins to feel guilty for ignoring him.

Please be strong. If you ignore the call for room service at night, within a few nights, your child will go back to sleep all night long without any more separation anxiety.

Remember that you can always use the video/audio monitor the check on your child's well-being without actually leaving your room.

DAY TIME NAPS:

When the child gets closer to 2-3 years of age, the number of daytime naps will diminish significantly, often to only one mid-afternoon nap.

SPHERE 2: BEHAVIORAL

In the next chapter I will discuss the terrible twos in greater detail. However, some elements of the child's struggle to control the adults around him will begin to be noticeable at this stage, in particular whining, temper tantrums, and aggressive behavior.

The recommendations I give in the next chapter apply to this age too.

Basically, when your child is whining, or having a temper tantrum, you should be very careful not to give in.

Remember whining and temper tantrums are like merchandise your toddler is trying to sell. If he realizes that his parents give in into this behavior, your child will begin behaving this way all day long, creating a nightmare situation for you.

However, if your child learns that you do not give in, and most importantly you completely ignore this behavior, the behaviors will soon stop.

Regarding aggressive behavior, when your child hits, bites or pulls your hair for the first time, you must react immediately and apply the Triple Response discussed in greater detail in the next chapter.

Do not think that this aggressive behavior is not intentional and do not laugh or ignore it. Immediately apply the three steps of the triple response.

First: establish eye contact with an angry facial expression;

Second: make a threatening move with your index finger;

Third: with a controlled but angry voice call your child by his full name and say aloud: "Do not hit/bite mommy." Immediately after, put the toddler down. Please do not console him when he starts crying. You do not console a child for hitting you.

If you don't stop this conduct immediately it will soon become a problem, and your child will start attacking other children. This could lead to isolation for your toddler and you, because few parents will allow their child to play with an aggressive play partner.

SPHERE 3: NUTRITIONAL

DIET FOR 15-24 MONTHS OF AGE

CONGRATULATIONS. Your baby is now ready to be part of the family table. By now she should be ready to try any kind of foods, EXCEPT for foods that the child has shown to be allergic to during the first six months of solid food, and food items that, because of their consistency, are not safe to be eaten, such as raw carrots, celery, steak, nuts, and hot dogs.

Whenever you try a new item, try it separately for five days before you incorporate it fully. Try to coordinate your meal schedule with your baby's. Your baby's menu should be as similar to yours as possible. By two years of age your baby could be capable of eating a similar quality and quantity of food as a bigger child.

MILK

Once the child is a year old, there is NO NEED for formula. You can switch to regular milk. (Consult with your pediatrician if there was a problem with milk allergy). The official recommendation of the AAP (American Academy of Pediatrics) is to provide whole milk three times daily to children between 12-24 months of age.

However, studies done in Europe showed that children in that age range that had an otherwise healthy diet with vegetables, fish, poultry, meats, and that consumed low fat milk twice daily, developed equally well as those children that used whole milk. If you give milk before any meal, the child's appetite will be significantly diminished. Please offer milk ONLY after a meal is completed.

Many baby formula companies want you to spend one more year on expensive follow up milk formulas. There is no need for you to spend money on those.

NUTRITIONAL SUPPLEMENTS

One trap that parents fall into very often is trying to make up for the picky eating habits of their children by providing nutritional supplements that claim to have the right nutrients, such as PediaSure, and similar products. If you give a healthy child any of those supplements, all you are achieving is teaching the child to be satisfied with thick chocolate milk with vitamins, with serious detrimental effects to creating healthy eating habits.

If the baby develops picky eating habits, you should follow the recommendations given in previous chapters. Basically, if your toddler refuses to eat her tuna salad with vegetables for lunch, finish your portion then remove the child's plate from the table.

DO NOT offer anything else but water until the following meal. Then offer the same food item as the previous meal. Keep on doing so until she eats anything you offer. Most children will give in within two or three meals.

SNACKING

MOTHER'S STASH OF ALL THE WRONG SNACKS

By 24 months of age, if you decide to provide snacks for your baby, you should be giving steamed broccoli, cauliflower, brussel sprouts, pickles, sliced almonds or cold cuts. You need to continue to avoid fruit juices, electrolyte drinks, cereals, cookies, yogurts, dehydrated fruits, and granola because no matter how organic or natural or fat free or vitamin loaded, those items are **pure carbohydrates, 100% sugar.**

PREVENTING PICKY EATING FROM 15 MONTHS TO 18 YEARS OLD

As you recall, picky eating habits could start as early as 9 months of age. Even in cases where a child is a great eater during the first few months after starting solid food, it is not a matter of if, but when your child will find that cereal, pasta, pretzels, cookies, and cakes tastes better. Again, it is human nature to prefer carbohydrates.

There are several factors that could ruin your success in teaching your child healthy eating habits.

1) Personality changes as the baby gets closer to 24 months of age. At this age, the child begins to experiment with sophisticated persuasive methods, such as whining, temper tantrums, sad looks, and false signs of affection. Do not give in. You know that your child is obviously clever, and capable of manipulation. If you completely ignore the screaming, whining and begging, your child will learn that you do not buy that merchandise, and will eventually realize that all you care about is healthy nutritional habits.

2) Peer pressure. One of the most difficult challenges for young parents is to be able to survive the pressure that Crystopper parents place on them.

When a mother goes out to the park, or any social program for babies, and 98% of the children are drinking apple juice, eating cheerios, goldfish cookies, etc., and she is told by the other mothers that it is "cruel" not to allow her child to "share" the junk food that the rest of children are eating, it makes the parent feel guilty to the extent that she might give in and offer junk food.

In my experience, a situation like this is a great opportunity to teach the other mothers a lesson about appropriate nutritional values. This would turn the tables around in such way that the other mothers would feel extremely guilty for feeding their children the wrong foods and snacks, and hopefully change their ways.

I have a patient that was following my advice with her two children. One was a toddler and the other one was a baby less than 12 months of age. She was so tired of her friends calling her "insensitive and cruel" that she made a DVD of her toddler eating healthy foods, going to sleep on her own, getting her breathing treatment for asthma on her own, etc.

My daughter-in-law, Susie, tells me how her friends cannot believe how my grandsons eat broccoli, brussel sprouts, cauliflower, sardines, herring, etc. Many of her friends are even beginning to follow in her footsteps.

3) Ability to reach for food. As children grow taller, they can help themselves to food items in the refrigerator or pantry. It is very important, for safety as well as health reasons, not to allow young children to have access to food by themselves. Keep any tempting foods out of sight.

As the child gets older (usually elementary school and older) and you trust their ability to serve themselves food, make sure that you have plenty of green vegetables, protein, tree nuts (almonds, pecans, walnuts, etc.) and water or non-caloric beverages. Please make sure they do not have access to bread, crackers, cereals, pasta, etc.

4) Adults and older siblings. A very common problem in many households is that babysitters, neighbors and family members, such as grandparents or adult siblings, feel sorry for the sad

looking child begging for the wrong snacks, and secretly provide those items for them.

BASIC RULE to remember: *IF YOU LOVE THEM, DO NOT FEED THEM WRONG FOODS.*

Chapter VIII

AGE 24 MONTHS TO THREE YEARS

THE TERRIBLE TWOS

Your child is now between 24 months to three years old. Hopefully you followed the instructions discussed in the previous chapters. As mentioned before in the introductions, there are "The Three Areas that Require 100% Parental Control."

1) SLEEP

Your child should be able to: go to bed by himself, and stay in bed all night without any kind of room service. Also, during the day time, your child should be able to take scheduled naps without any persuasion.

It is ok to have a bed time routine, such as storytelling, singing, praying, etc. However, once that activity is done, you should stand up, blow a kiss, and leave the room. Do not fall for any given excuse for you to stay any longer, such as, "I am thirsty," "I have to go to the bathroom," etc. The child should be taken to the bathroom and given any liquids **prior** to going to bed.

Under no circumstances should you allow your children to sleep in your bed. Likewise do not sleep in their room.

I

TRANSITION FROM CRIB TO BED

The right age to transition a child from a crib to a bed is approximately 24-36 months. The most common determining factor is the child's ability to climb over the crib's rail. Typically, it is very hard for a child younger than 2 years of age to do so. However, I have seen toddlers that were able to climb out of a crib as early as 18 months.

If you suspect that your child is even attempting to go over the crib's rail, take the necessary safety precautions to prevent any injuries. First, remove from the crib any object that could be used as a step, such as the cushion that surrounds the rails. Second, place a few pillows and blankets on the floor to prevent any major injuries in case of a fall.

Another reason to transition a child from a crib into a bed is the arrival of a new sibling. If the older child is close to 24 months old, it is a good idea to have him participate in the process of choosing big kid furniture. That will create a sense of being a big kid, not a baby, and will make the new bed easier to accept. Do not forget to buy removable safety rails.

A question that is in every parent's mind is, "What should I do if the child gets out of bed?" There are different possibilities:

1) The child will feel proud of having matured into a big kid bed and will stay in the bed without any problem.
2) The child will attempt to break free because he is no longer confined by a crib.

In the latter case, it is very important to teach the child that staying in bed at bedtime is non-negotiable. At the child's very first attempt to leave the bed, you should immediately take the child back to bed. Be firm, don't be apologetic.

The child must understand that staying in bed is mandatory. No matter how often the child attempts to leave the bed, you **must** take the child back to bed. If you are persistent, within a few days the child will not challenge you again. Some parents, out of frustration or fatigue, will give in and allow the child to stay in bed with them. This would be the biggest mistake you could ever make.

BEHAVIORAL

By age two, your child has developed a very sophisticated list of likes and dislikes. Children at this age make very accurate assessments of all the adults in their environment, their weaknesses and strengths.

The two-year old knows how to exploit each person's weak spots. They also know how to achieve their biggest successes using different tools:

- whining
- temper tantrums
- fake kisses and hugs aggressive behavior i.e. hitting, biting, hair pulling, throwing food or other items
- disobedience

WHINING

At approximately nine months of age, a baby learns that some adults are susceptible to annoying monotonous and repetitive sounds. Therefore, they use this whining to succeed in the business of obtaining everything they want.

Often I see older children in elementary and middle school, who in the classroom are recognized by everyone as mature students, but the moment they arrive home, transform themselves into whining monsters.

They do so because at home they have managed to open such a successful whining business, that they see no need to close it. Please do not allow the development of such behavior. If you do NOT give in, your child will have to declare bankruptcy, and will stop this annoying practice.

The solution applies for both whining and non-aggressive temper tantrums—ignore this behavior. When you give in to the child's demands, establish eye contact, or try to give a time out, you lose. If you are in a child safe room, you may walk away, or you can become busy doing something else. This will teach the child that there are no buyers for this behavior, and after failing to obtain benefits, this behavior will significantly diminish and eventually disappear.

TEMPER TANTRUMS

Children as young as one year old are capable of throwing temper tantrums. Temper tantrums are similar to whining in that they are triggered with the intention to manipulate the surrounding adults. Temper tantrums are more acute, louder, and sometimes more difficult to ignore than whining because of their complexity.

TYPICAL TEMPER TANTRUMS—The most typical type of temper tantrums goes through three stages.

Stage 1

When the child realizes that the adults taking care of him are not obeying or complying with the child's orders and commands, the child utilizes the first stage of a temper tantrum which is typically a sad face, tears, whining or sobbing. When parents devote their lives to become Crystoppers, their child is 100% convinced that the only purpose for the adults' existence is to placate him. Stage 2 starts if the adult fails to conform to the child's expectations.

Stage 2

At this stage, the sobbing and whining continue, but now the child is crying loudly, pretending to be desperate, often holding onto his parents' clothing. If the parents continue to fail to give in to the child's demands, then the temper tantrum enters Stage 3.

Stage 3

This is the "stage of no return." At this stage the child is so upset because of the parents' refusal to comply with his demands, that his anger causes him to forget the initial reason for the temper tantrum. Often the tantrum continues till the child is exhausted, sometimes even to the extent of falling asleep.

SOLUTION

In order to stop temper tantrums, simply follow the following suggestions: (See the solution for whining)

a. Ignore this behavior by not even establishing eye contact.
b. Under no circumstance should you give in to the child's wishes. Doing so is a grave mistake as the child will use this behavior

more frequently, in every situation where he does not obtain a satisfactory response.

c. Do not threaten or apply any punishment. Simply ignore the temper tantrum. Be strong. It is more damaging, with significant consequences, if you give in.

FAKE HUGS AND KISSES

Some children realize that one parent or family member loves to be hugged and kissed. They know that daddy, mommy, or grandpa or grandma will instantly melt with a hug or kiss. This melting behavior from an adult gives the child even better control than whining or screaming.

AGGRESSIVE BEHAVIOR

Most children will show, at some point, physical aggression towards the adults and family members caring for them. This is the end result of parents being Crystoppers instead of wise parents. Therefore, we need to understand why such young children would attack a person bigger and stronger than they are. There are a variety of reasons.

A) LEADER OF THE HOUSE

When the adults taking care of the child devote all their efforts and energy towards her happiness and consider it a goal to ensure she is never sad or crying, the child's perception is that the only purpose of existence for all the people around is to give in to her wishes. Therefore, when a parent does not conform, in the child's mind they deserve to be punished.

B) PERCEPTION OF STRENGTH

When a child is convinced that he is stronger than the surrounding adults, there is a distortion of perception of strength. For example, in the jungle, a small animal will never attempt to attack a lion or an elephant. This is the very basic principle of the law of the jungle. Only among humans, mainly in the last few decades, we see adults being victims of parental abuse. (See chapter on Parental Abuse).

It is very troublesome and heartbreaking to see how children of all ages physically and verbally abuse their parents. Many times I see that only one parent is abused and not the other. The reason why this happens has nothing to do with love. It is simply the survival of the fittest.

SOLUTION TO UNDERSTAND THE INSTINCT OF SELF-PRESERVATION

When a young child accidentally touches the fire of a candle and, as a consequence, suffers a minor burn, we can be sure that it is extremely unlikely that he will touch a fire under similar circumstances. When a child, regardless of age, begins to purposely hit, pull hair, bite, etc., and the adult's reaction is appropriate, this will probably be the beginning and the end of such behavior.

Therefore, it is very important to immediately stop any behavior that puts the parents, or the siblings or the child in physical danger as a result of hitting, pinching, kicking, running away, throwing objects, etc.

In order to do so, you must not justify such behavior by trying to rationalize aggression or saying, "he is too tired," "he is frustrated," "he cannot communicate," etc. Any kind of aggression is done on purpose with the intention to hurt. To stop it, use the **Triple Response**. The Triple Response consists of three actions that have to be done simultaneously.

A) Give your child a really angry look
B) Use an angry but firm and controlled voice. Call him by first and last name. Do not call him "darling, sweetie, honey, etc."
C) Wave your right index finger.

Immediately after the Triple Response you say: "Do not ever again do that again." Using a firm, controlled voice, send the child for a 20-30 minute time out. After the time out is over, you should act upset and angry for another 20-30 minutes.

WARNING: Be careful not to feel sorry when, after the triple response, your child suddenly starts to cry. If you console him, all your efforts will be in vain. If you feel guilty, your child will sense it and the triple response will be ineffective and the aggressive behavior will worsen.

You must be aware that in some areas, regulations call for expelling children that hit or bite frequently from day care or school. Parents will often not make play dates with aggressive children. It is in your and your child's best interest to teach the child that the behavior will not be tolerated.

DISOBEDIENCE

Disobedience is a consequence of parental Crystopping behavior.

When the child is educated such that the adults around him obey every single wish or when he is told "no" numerous times but the parent eventually relents, the obvious reaction is for the toddler to refuse to obey anything he is told, even when such behavior could be considered dangerous to the child.

One of the worst cases I saw in my practice involved a family with a newborn child and a two year old.

In my office there is a sign in each examining room asking parents not to allow their children to play with the medical supplies. When I walked in, I saw the two year old playing with a very pointy metal swab that was stored completely out of children's reach. The mother told me that she gave it to him because he was upset and "he wanted it."

I immediately took it away from the child.

I asked the mother how come she gave the child such a dangerous object to play with. She said that the child was crying too much and she could not handle it.

When I questioned her about providing the child with a potentially dangerous object that could have led to injury, she said that she was not worried because they were inside a pediatrician's office and the child could be "fixed" right away in case of an accident.

Disobedience is a form of aggression. The child is making a statement that she is stronger and in control. Regardless of the parents' input, the child's authority will prevail.

Parents have to decide which battles they want to fight. If the toddler prefers the blue shirt instead of the green one, let it be. Doing so will give the child a feeling that she is in control in some areas, but the parents actually control the important and significant aspects of the day to day life.

SOLUTION: It is very important for both parents to establish the rules they expect the child to follow. They also need to determine the immediate and long term consequences for a disobedient child. The parents' immediate reaction to disobedience will determine whether their authority will be respected or ignored at this age and into adulthood.

MEDICATIONS

Most parents hope that their children always remain healthy. Sooner or later, however, your child will catch a cold or suffer from an ear infection, bronchitis, etc.

Eventually you may have to give your child medications, breathing treatments or other therapeutic recommendations given by the pediatrician.

Unfortunately some medications don't taste good, and your child will not cooperate with you. Some children require breathing treatments given via nebulizer, nasal sprays, creams, ointments, etc. Often they will fight you all the way.

Remember that our job as parents is to do what is beneficial and avoid what is detrimental to your children. If you feel guilty and because of that you fail to provide the necessary medical treatment, you are actually harming your child.

In my opinion, one of the few situations when it is appropriate to bribe a child is for medication purposes. It is OK to distract the child with toys, movies, rewards, etc. You can even mix the medication with ice cream or other foods that the child prefers.

On occasion, you may need to give the medicine by immobilizing him and using a syringe designed for that purpose.

It is very important that, when in doubt, you call your pediatrician.

NUTRITIONAL

Even if you have been successful and your child has healthy eating habits, the terrible twos stage will present new challenges that will often catch you by surprise.

PEER PRESSURE

In this case, peer pressure not only applies to the way eating habits of the other children influence your toddler, but also to the comments that some other parents will make when they see your child drinking water instead of sugary drinks, or eating green vegetables or other healthy items as a snack instead of cookies, or other sugar loaded snacks.

Parents often call me because they are called cruel or mean by their friends and family for denying their child cookies and other junk food. It is an uphill battle to remain focused and remember the consequences of not instilling healthy eating habits during the first few years of life.

ABILITY TO REACH FOOD

This ability is the result of height. Once the child is tall enough to reach forbidden areas in the house, either by climbing onto chairs or by being able to open the pantry or the refrigerator, there is the possibility that she will attempt to independently take her favorite foods, especially the unhealthy kind.

MANIPULATION ABILITY

With the acquisition of language, your child is capable of manipulations. Manipulation becomes a tool to obtain food and control in the other two spheres, i.e. sleep and behavioral. Specifically, the skill of making faces, such as giving you puppy eyes or sad looks, or even saying painful things such as, "you don't love me" or "I hate you" etc.

It is amazing how even young children know the preferences of each adult in their world. For instance, they know that the mother may give in with a temper tantrum, that daddy may cave in with crying, and that the grandparents will melt with a smile and a hug.

SOLUTION

A) Parents eating habits must match what they tell their children to do. Until now, even if parents have unhealthy eating habits, they can still inculcate in their child healthy nutritional habits. However, as the child grows and acquires the ability to observe and learn, their parents' eating habits must match those that they advocate for their children.

B) Narrowing food choices does not prevent obesity. According to many experts, the factors that lead to obesity do not start at age 10 years or over; they start at age 24-36 months of age. The main reason is that as the child becomes more manipulative, and peer pressure builds both for care-givers and the child, the food variety begins to narrow.

The classical example to clarify how suddenly a good eater becomes a picky one is a triangle that has a very wide base, and an extremely narrow top. The wide base represents the first 12-18 months since the introduction of solid food. This is the easiest stage to achieve healthy eating habits by the use of conditioning behavior. If you do this correctly, you will be able to introduce a very large variety of green vegetables, protein, and fresh fruits. At the same time it is easy not to expose the child to junk food.

However, if you give in into your child's picky eating habits, by the time he reaches 2-3 years of age you will be looking at the triangle narrow with only a handful of food items that your child likes.

C) Do not give in to peer or social pressure. When the baby begins to socialize, he observes and learns the eating habits of 95% of surrounding children. At this point, parents may begin to feel guilty for depriving their children of all the candies, cookies, fruit juices and junk foods that other kids get. The rules begin to ease, and eating habits begin to deteriorate.

D) Fight back; educate other parents. Often I get phone calls from parents that feel very anxious about the continuous criticism from family and friends for not giving their children less healthy foods. It is understandable to feel that way when 95% of parents are instilling bad eating habits in their children and you are in the minority.

Instead of trying to be like them, educate them. Show them how your children eat broccoli, cauliflower, brussel sprouts, etc. Show them how they drink plain water instead of juices or sugary drinks. I have a parent that made a DVD showing her 2 year old daughter eating a large amount of vegetables, drinking water and taking her to bed without any struggle.

My son, Jonathan, and daughter-in-law, Susie, have many friends with children who are the same ages as theirs. When they see my grandchildren sleeping 10 uninterrupted hours at night, eating all green vegetables, drinking water, and behaving with respect, they tell them that they are very lucky to have such easy going children.

The reality is that my son and his wife are really committed to being wise parents and not Crystoppers. Many of their friends are beginning to apply similar principles with their children. Often friends and even strangers ask for advice on how to raise their children. In summary, they are helping others to be wise parents, and also creating an impact in their community.

CHAPTER IX

TOILET TRAINING

The precise age for toilet training varies from child to child. Often it is closely related to the child's language skills. Most children who can build 3-4 word sentences are toilet trainable. I have seen children completely trained by age 18 months while some are not trained until 36-42 months of age.

Other important factors are the commitment and willingness of the parents to start the training process and the presence of older siblings of the same gender.

EQUIPMENT

Numerous stores have toilet training potties and toilet seat adaptors. Some are mini-portable toilets were the child sits and pretends to be in a regular toilet seat. The disadvantage of these kinds of portable devices is that once you succeed with the training you have to begin a process of changing from the portable to the toilet seat adaptor. Therefore, it's best to bypass the small portable toilets and only use the toilet seat adaptors.

COMMITMENT AND WILLINGNESS

Often it is easier for some parents to continue the use of diapers during this process. While it seems easier, and is probably far less messy, as soon as your child sends signals that she is ready, you should go all the way. Do not fall in the trap of using the famous pull-ups. A pull-up is no different than a diaper. It could be, however, more expensive. So even though it no longer has the Velcro straps, it absorbs all humidity and your child does not even feel wet.

FIRST

You need to take the child to the toilet often. Eventually, it will coincide with the child's need to urinate or move her bowels. Once you succeed in doing so, it is okay to reward the child with a favorite treat.

You must be very careful to give only one very small treat. For example, a single mini-M&M is sufficient. If the treat is too large, the child's expectations for the next time will not be as powerful and his motivation will diminish.

You can establish two different levels of rewards. For example, when the child urinates, you give a small treat, but for a bowel movement, you can create a more appealing reward. Pick something your child really enjoys, such as a special toy or game or somewhere they like to go.

It is very important to have in mind that a child with an appropriate diet, rich in high protein and fiber, will be easier to toilet train because her bowel movements will be more regular and predictable.

A constipated child has no predictable patterns, and may even develop serious psychological problems as a result.

DIRECT REWARD SYSTEM

This system directly rewards a child for his willing participation in the toilet training process. When there is only one child at home, the reward process is the system that is most likely to be successful.

A) FOR URINATION

Set an alarm at two hour intervals to remind you to take the child to urinate. This has to take place wherever you happen to be, even if you are not at home. If your child tells you that, "I do not have to go," take her to sit on a toilet anyway.

Obviously, you have to take rewards with you so that you can immediately give them to your child. After being successful for two weeks, stop the rewards. Your child will already be used to being a big kid, will no longer enjoy being wet or in a diaper, will hopefully be proud of the accomplishment and will no longer need an external reward.

B) FOR BOWEL MOVEMENTS

In the early stages of toilet training, you need to establish a pattern of the child's bowel movements and sit him on the toilet at that specific time. Find entertaining games such a small puzzles, portable toys, story books, etc. to encourage your child to sit and relax for a while. The goal is to make the child comfortable on the toilet seat. Once he succeeds, you must immediately use the more appealing reward, one that will make the child feel he has really accomplished something worthwhile.

It's a good idea to place the reward in the bathroom in a very visible but unreachable spot. When the child has a bowel movement, take out the toy for only a few minutes. When he begins to enjoy playing with the toy, place it back in the original place. This will create a state of continuous expectation that will motivate the toddler to look forward to having a bowel movement. The child will also respond to seeing the happiness reflected in the parents' face when he is successful in the toilet training process.

As with urination, after a few weeks of success, stop the rewards system because the child will then feel more comfortable using regular dry and clean underwear. It is totally appropriate for the first few weeks to let the toddler sleep with a night time diaper.

INDIRECT REWARD SYSTEM

This system does not directly reward a child for going to the bathroom. However, it creates a strong desire to be toilet trained to catch up to an older sibling. Obviously this method requires that the older sibling is willing to participate and is more effective if the older sibling is the same gender as the younger one.

A) FOR URINATION

You must find three days when you know you and the older sibling are ready to work together to toilet train the younger one. As with the direct method, you will use a reward that the younger sibling loves. However, in this case you will make sure that when the older child goes to the bathroom the younger one is watching.

As soon as the older child washes her hands, give the older child the reward that the younger child loves. When the younger one sees that the older sibling got a reward that she wants, she will immediately demand to receive the same. All you need to do then is to tell the younger one, "He got the reward because he made on the toilet."

Once you repeat this scenario every two hours, even without been asked the younger one will go to the bathroom and start urinating on her **own** initiative. From that point on, continue the direct rewards for a few weeks.

B) FOR BOWEL MOVEMENTS

Follow the same principle as for urination but make the reward that much more appealing. You have to make sure that the younger one is watching the entire scenario.

Even though the frequency of bowel movements is not the same as urination, over a period of two or three days you will have the opportunity to create an overwhelming desire in the child to play with that very attractive toy. Soon the younger child will be fully toilet trained.

NIGHT TIME BED WETTING (Enuresis)

Day time bladder control is not related to night time bed wetting. It is a condition the child has no control over. During the first few months of the toilet training process, your toddler may experience day time and night time accidents.

However, if the child stops having day time accidents but continues to have nighttime accidents then you need to consider the possibility that he has enuresis.

Obviously, you should try to improve the situation by taking the following steps:

A) Decrease the amount of fluid consumed before bed time.
B) Try to take the toddler to the bathroom (even half asleep) between 10 PM to 12 midnight.

Often, even if you do the above mentioned suggestions, the child will continue to be a bed wetter. This medical condition called *enuresis* is caused by a specific diminished night time secretion of the anti-diuretic hormone and is a hereditary problem. If you investigate you will probably find a family member that was a bed wetter for years, sometimes into the teens.

If your child has enuresis, discuss this condition with your pediatrician. Even though enuresis will improve without intervention, it is impossible to know when. It could disappear at age 4 or last until age 10 or more. Because bed wetting could affect a child's self-esteem, there are several options for medical treatment that range from night time bed wetting alarms all the way to anti-diuretic hormone supplements, or even bladder control medications.

Carry extra underwear, plenty of wipes and an extra set of clothing. Do not punish or offend the child for accidents. Be patient and continue positive enforcement.

REGRESSION

Sometimes, a fully toilet trained child will regress. This could happen as a result of several circumstances such as family tensions, divorce, moving **to a new home,** the start of school or a new babysitter. It is quite common for the arrival of a new sibling to cause regression usually as a result of the child's desire to gain attention or control of the situation.

The jealous toddler, realizing that the new baby is changed often, desires the same attention and feels they have lost their place and therefore finds a way to regain his position. Sadly, many adults are fully convinced that when a new baby arrives, there is a need to make it up to the older child and they ease up on basic discipline.

As will be discussed in the next chapter, it is vital to continue with the same behavioral rules. If you put a diaper back on previously toilet trained child, it could be years before you can regain control.

CHAPTER X

NEW SIBLINGS

The arrival of a new brother or sister can be very destabilizing for a family. Even if you have followed the rules discussed in the previous pages, the truth is that in many parents' minds, the first child is the center of the universe and rules the house.

In our society, it is very common to welcome the birth of a new baby by also buying gifts for the older child. Typically, this is done because of the guilty feelings that family members have regarding how difficult the transition will be for the child.

There is a general concern that the older sibling will feel displaced or less loved with the arrival of a new baby. In order to make up for the new baby, they bribe the older children at home by saying, "These presents were given to you by the new baby."

Obviously, even young toddlers understand that it is physically impossible for a newborn baby to bring presents. The children then realize the adults around them are worried about his reaction to the new sibling, and they also notice that the daily discipline routine is not strictly enforced. Therefore they learn that the parents can be manipulated and regress in order to capitalize on their guilt.

REGRESSION

Toddlers will try to regress by imitating their newborn siblings. They act that way in order to maintain the level of control at home, which is their territory, and they will do so with the expectation of reconquering their lost kingdom. In their mind, the newborn gets more attention because they cry, require diaper changes, etc.

When they see the level of attention the new baby gets, it brings back memories of the times when they got 100% of their parent's attention.

The regression may occur in several areas.

TOILET TRAINING REGRESSION

As discussed in the toilet training chapter, this area could also be affected by a new baby. The fully toilet trained child will try to regain control by going back to diapers. By doing so, the child thinks that they will again get their parents' undivided attention and that the new baby will be forgotten.

As mentioned before, do not, under any circumstances, allow the older child to regress. Simply continue with the same level of discipline you had at home before the arrival of the new baby.

SPEECH REGRESSION

A child that was previously using mature language will suddenly begin to use baby talk. Not only will they stop building sentences, but they will also use an infantile tone of voice.

It is always important to talk to your children in a normal, adult, mature voice. But when you notice that the older sibling regresses and starts to imitate a baby voice, you have to immediately tell him that until he speaks in a normal voice, you will not be able to respond to him.

SLEEP REGRESSION

The older child should be able to sleep all the way through the night by age six months. When he sees that the new sibling is up late at night and early in the morning, there may be an attempt to obtain room service at these hours as well.

Even if there is a need to have the new baby share a room with an older child, the older child does not require protection or isolation from the crying of the new baby at night. After a few days, the older child will filter out the crying and will learn to sleep despite the noise.

It is known that people that move near the train tracks, after a few days, are able to filter the noise and vibration from the train. Even if the train uses its horn, the inhabitants of those homes are able to completely filter the noise and not wake up at all.

BEHAVIORAL REGRESSION

The toddler may attempt to use old tricks that had been successful in the past, such as temper tantrums, whining, aggressiveness, etc.

Many parents and family members may give in because they feel guilty that the older child is upset about the arrival of the new baby. Please follow the rules mentioned before. If you give in and act on your guilt, you will create a serious behavioral issue that will only get worse.

NUTRITIONAL REGRESSION

When the older child realizes that everybody at home is busy and distracted by the new baby, he will begin to ask for treats that are usually not permitted. It is far too easy to give in at moments like these. Prepare healthy food in advance, particularly for when you will be in the hospital, and ensure that the child and other family members follow the same rules while you are less available.

CHAPTER XI

DAY CARE

These days, more and more parents are taking advantage of the option to put their child in day care. One reason is that financial necessity requires both parents to work outside the home. For single parents, the need for day care is even more pressing.

The ideal situation, particularly for young babies, would be to be cared by responsible family members, which would avoid the baby's exposure to numerous other children and the increased risk of contracting illness. Even if this is not an option in your home, caution in choosing a day care is advised. Not all day care centers are licensed and the staff who care for the children are not always well-trained. Children cared for by sitters who are not trained or in facilities that are not licensed face many dangers, both physical and psychological.

Regardless of who is doing the baby sitting, parents need to be very specific in giving instructions to those taking care of their babies. Parents need to specify the importance of healthy foods, and instruct those in charge to avoid the extremely unhealthy snacks that 90% of children are given on a daily basis. Those unhealthy, sugar-loaded foods include fruit juices, cereals, fish cookies, etc. Ideally, parents should bring food from home to the day care center or provide a detailed list, in writing, of what the child is allowed to have.

AGE 3 TO SIX YEARS

For this age, the three spheres, or areas of behavior, mentioned in the previous chapters, from the first year of life until age three, continue to be similar. However, there are a few new factors that come with the child getting older and more mature. The challenges of parenting increase significantly with every year.

At this age, family members and baby sitters are involved in the daily care of the child. Many children start to attend school and begin to interact with teachers. Parents must be aware of their child's new manipulative abilities that come with experience and especially from having learned the strengths and weaknesses of the people in charge at home or at the day care center.

PRE-K SCHOOL

For many children, attending school is a traumatic event because they are no longer the ruler of their house. This is particularly true for the eldest child in a family.

In school, the child becomes part of a social group with 10 to 25 other individuals. They all need to follow the teachers' rules and learn to participate in and work with a team. Hopefully, a good teacher will establish herself as a leader on the first day and teach the young student to learn to work with others.

The child's speech will also improve because, in order to be understood by his peers, he must speak clearly and increase his vocabulary. My opinion is that for the typical child, pre-k school provides the best and most effective speech therapy.

THREE BEHAVIORAL SPHERES FOR CHILDREN 3-6 YEARS OLD

SPHERE 1—SLEEP

Children older than three have different sleep needs. A great majority still need a midday nap. It is recommended that you follow similar guidelines as discussed in the three spheres in Chapters I and VIII.

There is, however, a big difference in speech at this stage. By age three, most children have acquired a large vocabulary and even the ability to build complex sentences.

It is wonderful to see how quickly a child's vocabulary grows and develops and how beautifully children can express themselves. It is a great relief to parents to be able to have more elaborated conversations with their child and the vast increases in intellect and ability that comes along with that.

However, speech also increases the child's ability to manipulate and even blackmail parents. Therefore, it is very important to establish a bed time routine for your child. Make sure that before sending your child to bed you have taken care of all the possible reasons for the child to be out of bed—snack, drinks, bathroom, fear of the dark, etc. Once all of that is complete you can begin the bedtime routine.

BEDTIME ROUTINE: After following the above mentioned steps, do a very routine, quiet, peaceful activity such as reading a bed time story or singing a quiet bedtime song. Then give the child a kiss and leave the room.

BEDTIME MISTAKES

Once you leave the room, do not fall for any trap like, "I'm still thirsty," "lay down next to me," etc. The most serious of all mistakes is to let your child sleep with you in the same bed. Letting her to get used to sleeping in your room could have terrible consequences in the present and immediate future. This behavior could affect your relationship with your spouse, and affects the child's self-esteem.

If she says, "I am scared," explain in detail that there is no reason to be afraid, and if necessary leave a small light on. But don't fall for the same trick over and over. After the first time, just do the bed time routine and leave the room.

SPHERE 2: BEHAVIORAL

Behavioral issues change significantly at this stage. In chapter VIII I mentioned that during the first 36 months of life, almost any challenge in the three spheres (i.e. sleep, behavioral, nutritional) can be solved with conditioning behavioral modification.

At age three, the child has developed new skills and communication methods. They already have their own personality. They already have chosen favorite toys, games, foods, activities, etc.

Regarding the people that are part of the child's life, she already knows the weak and strong attributes of each of the surrounding adults. She knows how to extract the maximum benefit from each person.

For example, the child may learn that the mother will break after whining or temper tantrums and that the father will melt with a hug or a kiss. Often there are other adults closely involved in the child's care. Grandparents and baby sitters may also play a major role in the upbringing of many children.

As time goes by, the principle of "divide and conquer" becomes part of the child's method of manipulation. At this stage, disobedience should be approached the same way as aggressive behavior. Parents should establish, in advance, the different levels of punishment and withdrawal of privileges for each transgression. Failing to enforce these punishments could cause rebellion and aggression all the way into adulthood.

MANIPULATION PREVENTION

It is very important for all the adults to be consistent in analyzing and acting on every aspect of the child's behavior. **Do not forget that by uniting, you are not joining forces against the child, but preventing serious future health and social problems.**

DISCIPLINE FOR CHILDREN 3-6 YEARS OLD

At this age, there is an element that was not present in the younger child: dialogue. Most children that belong to this age group are capable of understanding what their parents consider to be wrong. They can sense what makes their parents happy or upset. Therefore, using different approaches, they can be taught the concept of consequences for their actions.

1) TIME OUT

This method is used for minor transgressions. You have to choose a room in the house, ideally not the child's own bedroom, but it can be used if necessary. Like the name "time out" suggests, establish an average of 20 minutes.

During this time, remove from the room any toy, game or distraction that could make it enjoyable for the child to be in the room. Try to make the time out an experience that the child will not look forward to in the future.

2) PRIVILEGES WITHDRAWAL; CREATING FAMILY GUIDELINES

At this stage, most parents are aware of what their children look forward to, what they dislike the most, what are their favorite activates toys and games, best friends, etc.

Since children at this age understand what their parents do not want them to do, and they comprehend the concept of punishment and reward, it is appropriate for parents to have scheduled meetings a few times a month and evaluate their performance as parents.

At the same time, parents should separately analyze the behavior of each child and create a list of urgent items that need to be fixed. It is very important not to forget the concept that the "punishment must fit the crime."

A list must be created based on ranking order of the severity of the child's transgression. Then put in writing the action that both parents agree will be the response for misbehavior. Once a list that clearly and concisely defines what the punishment will be for each transgression is created, a private meeting with the child should be scheduled.

The meeting should be held individually with each child, without any interruptions or distractions. First, it is important to mention the positive attributes of the child. Then immediately, in a very serious, clear way, describe to your child the different wrongdoings you have noticed and the EXACT punishment he will get in case of breaking the rules again.

Make sure the child repeats, word by word, the rewards of listening to you as well as the consequences of inappropriate behavior. Once this is done, make him sign the paper with a crayon, or a stamp, or a sticker.

APPLYING FAMILY GUIDELINES

In order to successfully apply the punishment part of the family guidelines, we have to act in a similar way that the police do to adults who break traffic rules. For example, when we run a red light, our first punishment is the flashing police car lights. Obviously, we cannot tell the police officer that we were not aware that we had to stop at the red light because we were taught the traffic rules when we obtained a driver's license. Then, as the second part of the punishment we get a traffic ticket that will force us to either pay the ticket, or to hire a lawyer. As if that was not enough, the third part of the punishment is that points are applied to our driver's license and our car insurance rates go up.

Using a similar approach, when a child purposely breaks the rules given to him, you must immediately apply the:

1) Initial punishment
Being sent to the room, being grounded, losing privileges, etc. This initial punishment has to be strong and effective. Do not forget that the child received a warning. In our current electronically oriented society, children enjoy computer and video games and activities as much as

previous generations enjoyed TV. For many children watching Sesame Street, Barney, Thomas the Train, Dora the explorer, etc., is a very important part of their daily activities.

Even though some of these shows and games are educational in nature, the child would not be happy if, because of misbehavior, he was not allowed to enjoy his shows or play his games. Therefore, removal of these constitutes a very effective initial punishment.

2) Follow up punishment

After the initial punishment shock is over, the child needs to be reminded about his misbehavior. Therefore, it is OK to follow up with a minor reminder, such as a few days of no dessert or bike riding.

3) Long term punishment

This punishment stage should last a few days, or even weeks after the initial and follow up punishments. It should be applied particularly when the child is defiant and disobedient. For example, one or two weeks without after school recreational activities, dessert, video games, etc. It is important to choose the appropriate punishment in order to ensure that the child will think twice next time before misbehaving.

SPHERE 3: NUTRITIONAL

At this stage, age 3-6 years old, parents will face a bigger challenge in order to continue to provide healthy nutritional habits. Most pre-K schools are privately funded and therefore need to save money and keep parents happy. It is cheaper to buy pasta, bread, crackers, cereals and fruit juice, than poultry, tuna, vegetables, etc.

We discussed in previous chapters that carbohydrates taste better than nutritious foods, and for obvious reasons children prefer those. Because of that, when the child returns home from pre-K, the official teacher's report will likely state that the child ate very well.

What the teacher does not say is that the child drank large quantities of fruit juice (i.e. sugar), ate cereal and lots of fish cookies, crackers, etc.

Sadly, the combination of inexpensive, unhealthy foods and snacks is accepted by everybody, and that is how good eating habits go down the drain. As a parent that pays tuition, you should demand to be the one choosing what your child eats, even if you have to send all the food and snacks to school every day. You could also become a volunteer in the school's PTA and help establish healthy guidelines for school food purchasing. But the most important point is not to give in to the eating habits of your child's peers.

CHAPTER XII

ELEMENTARY SCHOOL

Elementary school children are real people with their own personalities, preferences, goals, and social groups. Raising children is a very difficult job. Parents can be successful in some battles, but should never think they have won the war.

The three behavioral spheres are still very important.

SPHERE 1: SLEEP

If you succeeded in teaching your child good sleeping habits, the child in elementary school age could easily become a very good sleeper. It **is very important that your child to go to bed calm and relaxed.**

Do not, under any circumstances, install a television in your child's bedroom. Also, make sure that he has no access to video games, computers or any electronic devices that may prevent him from falling asleep.

Make every effort to ensure your child sleeps 8-10 hours.

SPHERE 2: BEHAVIORAL

At this age, behavioral issues change. Obviously, if you were successful in teaching your child that whining and temper tantrums lead nowhere, this type of behavior should not be a problem. You now have a new set of school and social issues to enforce while still making sure that your child respects parental authority and the rules of discipline.

Make sure you establish, in advance, what it is that you expect from your child. This includes specific time for homework, recreation and electronic activities that are educational and non-violent. At this stage you have to continue the reward and removal of privileges system. However, your expectations are different. You want your child to be a good, responsible student, socially respectful, and a good listener.

A very effective punishment at this age is grounding screen time (i.e. TV, video games, and computer). Nothing will motivate a child to comply with parental requests as much as the potential loss of screen time.

If you allow your child to watch TV or play video games, make sure that they are age-appropriate and non-violent.

Remember, at this stage you can have periodic meetings with your child and openly let her know the behavioral issues that need improvement. Specify in advance consequences for not complying with your rules and requests.

SPHERE 3: NUTRITIONAL

Nutritional issues intensify at this age because of the increase in social activities. On top of attending birthday parties, some children go to sleepovers at friends' homes.

This kind of social activities will expose your child to the 90% of the pediatric population that has very poor eating habits, and obtains 90% of their caloric intake from carbohydrates alone.

Obviously, it is impossible to ask a child not to eat cake or other junk food at a party or social event. Therefore, allow your child to partake of those food items, with the clear understanding that this is only an exception to the rule. Continue to be a good role model for your child regarding life style and healthy habits.

TAKING YOUR CHILD TO THE SUPERMARKET

Elementary school age children are capable of understanding basic principles of healthy eating.

Whenever you go grocery shopping, take your older children with you. Over a short period of time she will learn to choose the right fruits and vegetables. In my household, I have done grocery shopping for as long as I can remember. When my now adult children were younger I took them to the supermarket with me as often as possible. Now as adults, they are able to make wise decisions in their grocery shopping on a day to day basis.

WARNING: please do not become one of those Crystoppers parents we see in the supermarket every day that buy their child everything they want just because they cry and scream.

TAKING YOUR CHILD TO A RESTAURANT

It is very important to try to maintain a consistent lifestyle with your children, even when you are out in a restaurant or on vacations. You can allow the family to have some special treats while at a restaurant, but try to maintain some structure. Make sure you send away the bread basket that is served until the child has eaten vegetables and protein. Make sure that the adults do the same. Try to AVOID SODAS or sweet drinks while you are at the restaurant. Obviously, for dessert you can allow the family to have something different like cookies or ice cream.

TAKING YOUR CHILD TO A BIRTHDAY PARTY OR SOCIAL EVENT

Before you get to the party, explain to your child that special social events are an exception to the rule and that she can eat anything there. Official studies have shown that eating a lot of sugar loaded products does not cause hyperactivity. However, in my experiences as a pediatrician since 1980, I have clearly noticed a significant change in some children when they eat candies or drink fruit juices. I remember quite well when my older grandson, at his first birthday, ate cake for the first time. He was so hyper he could not stop running around.

CHAPTER XIII

PRE TEEN AND TEENAGE YEARS

Regarding the different levels of difficulty of educating children, teenage years are the most challenging of all. If you failed to take the right steps in educating your child the right way in all the spheres, your family will now be facing a serious crisis.

SPHERE 1: SLEEP

Teenagers experience an accelerated growth rate, almost as impressive as during the newborn period. Therefore, they require many hours of sleep, at least 8 hours. However, the opposite is what tends to happen. Teenagers are so busy, that many sleep less than five hours. Even when they go to bed they are up until the wee hours of the morning listening to music, text messaging, surfing the internet, sending email, twittering or updating facebook pages.

In the morning they are exhausted, without the will or energy to fulfill their school duties, and still thinking only of their social activities.

Because of that, it should not be a surprise that our high school graduates read at the level of elementary children, and cannot succeed in a competitive professional world.

As a parent, you must restrict and control your teenager's access to those electronic devices, even if you get a mouthful of accusations, and statements regarding on how they are no longer babies, or how you don't respect them as grownups, etc.

Please do not give in and vigilantly implement the sleep rules at all cost. You will be rewarded when you see your teen getting good grades and functioning better in daily tasks.

SPHERE 2: BEHAVIORAL.

As parents, the biggest challenge you will ever face is your children's teenage years. Teenagers are children in adult bodies. Therefore, physically they can do the same activities as any adult, but they lack the maturity of an older person. Because of that they are prone to become engaged in very risky and dangerous behavior.

1) Alcohol consumption, tobacco and drug use.
Statistically some studies show that up to 75% of high school students become involved with alcohol or drugs at some point, and up to 90% of them said that they were offered drugs or alcohol. Tobacco smoking is more frequently seen among teenagers than adults.

Because of the above mentioned statistics, there is a disproportionate rate of car accident related fatalities with teenagers as compared to the general population. To make things worse, in some states a teenager can obtain a driver's license at age 16.

WHAT YOU SHOULD DO

a. Talk to your children about the dangers of drugs, tobacco and alcohol as early as middle school, and lead by example.
b. Buy a breathalyzer device; they are easily available online. Your teenager should know that you are going to randomly administer a breathalyzer, even if their behavior doesn't seem to warrant it.
c. Ask your telephone company about a GPS-like service that allows you to know your teen's location at all times as well as and at what speed he is driving.
d. Do not allow your teenage driver to have more than two passengers at one time. Having more passengers in the car may cause distraction, and increase the risk of a car accident.
e. Demand that the parents of each potential passenger give you a notarized letter in which they assume full responsibility for any

injury that their child may sustain as a passenger in your child's car. Doing so may save you years of lawsuits and headaches.

f.   Buy over the counter drug testing kits that are capable of detecting the presence of drug substances in a urine sample. These are very accurate, and allow you to send a sample to the company and confirm your findings.

You may wonder if taking the above mentioned steps will lead to a relationship of distrust between you and your teenager. Actually that is what your adolescent child will want you to believe, and he will try to make you feel guilty about implementing basic rules.

Some of the arguments you will hear are, "You don't love me anymore," "how could you do this to me," "you know me; I would never smoke, drink or break the law," etc. The majority of teenagers live in a world of their own, in which only other peers count as true friends, and only friends are worthy of their trust.

I am not saying that your teenager does not love you, but your teen will not tell you even half of what is going on in their mind or life, even if you have a good relationship with them. Your only goal is to keep them safe and away from harm. They need to know that even though they have grown into young adults, they have three major obligations as part of your contract with them.

CONTRACT

1)   Be respectful of their parents.
2)   Be compliant with their school duties and obtain the best grades possible.
3)   Stay away from trouble with drugs, alcohol, gangs and inappropriate sexual behavior.

You may wonder how you can enforce the contract to a child with a body of an adult. Obviously time out, threats and yelling do not work.

However there are many benefits that some teenagers take for granted such as money allowances, electronic devices such as computers, smart phones, portable music devices, clothing allowances, social outings, and the most important benefit for a teen, driving a car.

Without your financial support, your teen's life is ruined. If you ground your teen, remove their allowance or take the car away from them, you will see how quickly their behavior will change. You have to be strong and consistent. If the contract is broken, you have the right and obligation to revoke your teenager's benefits.

Like I mentioned before, you are going to be bombarded with accusations with the intent of making you feel guilty. Do not give in. Your reward will be to raise young, responsible adults who are able to find a career and become healthy, productive citizens. When this happens, and your children grow up, they will actually thank you.

TROUBLED TEEN

Sadly, many teens end up in trouble with the law, or with school because of drug and alcohol abuse. If you followed the recommendations mentioned before, (buying a breathalyzer, drug testing kits, etc.) and your teen tests positive, or you can see obvious signs of intoxication, you need to know that you are not alone. Don't be afraid to immediately find drug rehabilitation centers and support groups. You don't have the experience to fix addiction problems by yourself.

Also, don't believe your teen when he tells you that he will "never do it again." Remember, you have to act before your teen reaches the age of 18. After 18, you are not legally allowed to force your child into rehabilitation or therapy and it becomes more difficult to voluntarily send a child to any institution. At that point, the only way to do so is by getting the police to apply the Baker Act.

PSYCHIATRIC PROBLEMS

The transition from childhood to adulthood is very difficult. Teenagers are very prone to developing depression that may lead to suicide. Also eating disorders such as obesity, bulimia, or anorexia are prevalent at this age. If you suspect your child is having any psychiatric issue, don't be in denial; seek professional help as soon as possible.

SPHERE 3: NUTRITIONAL

If you have followed the recommendations given in previous chapters about how to teach your child a healthy nutritional life style, you will have an easier time continuing through the adolescent years.

Scientific studies done on overweight teenagers show that the main cause of obesity is not lack of exercise, but rather the lifestyle of the parents at home. Because 90% of all groceries in the house are purchased by a parent, the teenager consumes what you buy. Similar studies showed that overweight teenagers who did intense cardiovascular exercise with professional trainers without modification of the home dietary lifestyle did not lose any weight.

However, the studies confirmed that when parents established a healthy lifestyle at home, even without any exercise, teens lost their extra weight within a few months. Many parents think that if they place their teen on a diet there is a potential for eating disorders. This argument could be accurate if only one family member is forced to go on a diet rather than applying a healthy eating lifestyle for the entire family.

But if a healthy lifestyle is followed by all family members, regardless of their physical appearance, your teenager will not develop eating disorders because she is not singled out as the only fat family member.

If your teen has healthy eating habits, it is 100% thanks to you, the parent. The opposite is also true. Whether your teen is fat or thin, if he has bad eating habits, it is 100% your fault as well.

It is such a pleasure to see teenagers eating vegetables, fruits and healthy protein.

Obviously this kind of diet is the result of a healthy lifestyle that was instituted when the child was an infant.

As parents, you need to know that when you inculcate healthy eating habits in your children, you probably add 10-15 years to their adult lives.

TEENAGE OBESITY, DIABETES AND METABOLIC SYNDROME

Unfortunately, over the last decade, I have seen more obese teenagers that end up having medical conditions that years ago were exclusively found in adults. When I was in medical school in the 70's, we knew that there were two kinds of diabetics: Juvenile and the Adult Onset.

The juvenile onset diabetes, or Type I, is probably the result of some autoimmune condition, not related to obesity. Therefore, some children are diagnosed in the first few years of life.

Adult onset diabetes, or Type II, is the result of inappropriate eating habits and obesity together with a genetic predisposition. Sadly, I have seen many obese teenagers with inappropriate eating habits inculcated to them by their parents since they were toddlers. They subsequently develop Type II diabetes, high blood pressure, joint problems, etc.

These teenagers also suffer from low self-esteem that leads to social isolation, depression and even suicide. One of the most severe cases I saw in my practice was a 14 year old boy that came to the office for a sports physical examination. He was close to 70 pounds overweight, so the football coach wanted him to play defense on the team. His blood pressure was already abnormally high, and he had already developed Stage II diabetes.

Also, because of his size, he was unable to tolerate minimal exercise. The strangest part was that both parents that came with him to the office were in perfect shape—strong, muscular and athletic looking. I was told that they owned a fitness center. I was confused. How come the parents were so healthy and had such a healthy lifestyle, and yet allowed their son to become morbidly obese?

When I took them aside to talk in private, they told me that they provide a healthy diet at home based on protein, fruits, vegetables and healthy grains. However, they mentioned that their son was very picky since the age of two.

Because of his pickiness, they were so afraid that he would starve to death that they gave in and served him cereals, bread, pasta, fruit juices and all kinds of unhealthy snacks.

I instructed them on how to change their approach. Within a few weeks they were able to reverse the damage they had done to their son by completely removing the unhealthy food items from the home.

In summary, this was a rare case in which the parents had a very healthy lifestyle for themselves but not for their son.

This case supports the principle that it is NEVER TOO LATE to return to a healthy lifestyle.

NUTRITION FOR THE PATIENT TAKING ADHD MEDICATIONS

Many school age children and teens take medications to control their ADHD (attention deficit hyperactivity disorder).

Obviously you must make sure that your child was diagnosed by a professional psychologist or psychiatrist who did a thorough evaluation and has come up with an accurate diagnosis of ADHD.

Most medications that are used to treat this condition will significantly reduce the child's appetite. This appetite suppression is most significant at lunch time. When the medication starts to wear off in the afternoon, suddenly their appetite returns.

Unfortunately, because the child has not eaten very much since breakfast, the sudden burst of appetite will create an urge to eat unhealthy foods.

SOLUTION: In the morning, 20 minutes before taking the medication the child MUST EAT PROTEIN, and a carbohydrate, like fruit or whole grain bread. A study done in Florida showed that high school students that were given protein and fruit for breakfast scored 20% higher on their SAT test than their peers that either skipped breakfast or only ate a carbohydrate such as cereal, oatmeal, muffin, bagels, granola, etc.

The same study done in the adult population showed similar results. Adults that ate protein for breakfast were able to concentrate at work and perform their job better than those that ate only carbohydrates.

Since the goal for successful treatment of ADHD is to allow the patient to concentrate and perform their duty at school in a better way, it makes sense to implement a better diet in order for the medication to be more effective.

When your child comes back from school, let him have a healthy pre-dinner with protein, vegetables and fruits. Remove unhealthy snacks from the pantry.

If you don't enforce these recommendations, the medicine may not work and your child may even fail to grow to his maximum potential. Short stature is a complication of ADHD medications when the appropriate diet is not followed.

CHAPTER XIV

ADULTHOOD

Eventually, your child will leave home to go to college, or to get a job. If, over the first 18 years of your child's life, you followed the recommendations given in this book, you will find that your relationship with your child has now reached a new level.

Many parents think that once their child graduates college they've succeeded as parents and their job is done. I think that the job of being a parent never ends. Our children still need our help and guidance; they will need us when they build their own family. You have to be there to celebrate with them all of the happy occasions that life brings, and act as a support and resource during difficult times.

I have personally been blessed with a fantastic mother-in-law. When she was living outside the USA and we needed a last minute babysitter, she would take a plane and stay with our children. Anytime we had a new baby, she would do the same.

Her devotion did not end there. She has come to us anytime any of our grandchildren were born to help her grandchildren take care of her great-grandchildren.

Anytime there was a family illness or surgical procedure, she would come and stay as long as necessary.

Your young adults will need you to help them when they have their own children. However, don't try to impose your own views on how you expect your grandchildren to be educated. Give advice in a positive way, and work with them as partners.

A NOTE TO GRANDPARENTS

If you are fortunate enough to be a grandparent, be aware that your now adult children will need you to help them with their children, especially in an economy that requires a dual income. Therefore, if you are able to help them, please do so. Believe me, it will be one of the most rewarding experiences of your life.

Don't forget that if you spoil your grandchildren, you will cause chaos in their lives, and serious family problems for your children. Most of all, do not try to bribe your grandchildren with candies or presents, because you will undermine the efforts of their parents and they will try to take advantage of you without actually loving you.

Offer advice when it is asked of you, and otherwise trust that you have raised your children to make good, educated choices for theirs.

If you believe that there is some POSITIVE advice you must give them, do it in private and not in front of their children.

Your grandchildren will love you because of what you do for them in their daily lives, like babysitting, playing with them, doing homework, taking care of them when they are sick, etc.

In summary, be positive forces in their lives so that you are a source of love and a positive figure for them to look up to.

Notes

Notes

Notes

Notes

Notes

Notes

Notes

Notes

Notes

Notes

Notes

Notes

Notes

Notes

Notes

Notes

Notes

Notes

Notes

Notes

Notes

Notes

Notes

Notes

Notes

Notes

Notes

Notes

ABOUT THE AUTHOR

Dr. Kaweblum has been a pediatrician since 1980.

He is the father of three children and grandfather of two.

Dr. Kaweblum is actively involved in his community and he also has a black belt in Shoto-kan karate.

Born and raised in Mexico City, where he completed his first pediatric residence in Mexico City in 1983. Moved to the USA in 1983, where he completed a second residency in pediatrics at the University of Miami.

It was there where he became very interested in pediatric behavioral practice.

Together with his wife Yvette, founded in 1989 Boca Del Mar Pediatric and Adolescent Center in Boca Raton, FL.

He has been named Top South Florida pediatrician several times from 1997 to 2011, and Florida Super Doctor since 2008-2010 by key professional media. Also most highly regarded pediatricians of South Florida by Castle Connolly on seven occasions through 2010.

Over the last few decades he has noticed a very serious decline on the parent's ability to do their job. Children are disobedient, misbehaved and overweight.

The main reason: 95 per cent of parents devote all their energy to stop their children from crying; even if it means not to teach them the right sleeping skills, behavioral and nutritional values; instead they allow bad habits. That makes them "CRY-STOPPERS".

Dr. Kaweblum believes that in order to be a parent you have to follow three rules: 1.-If something is bad for your child don't do it. 2. - If it is good do it. (Regardless of crying whining, or hugging). 3. - Do not say I will try, just do it.

His goal is to teach parents on how to rise healthy, well behaved, nutritionally balanced and socially adapted children.

CPSIA information can be obtained at www.ICGtesting.com
Printed in the USA
LVOW110824051111

253614LV00001B/77/P